Now
That's
a GOOD
QUESTION!

Now That's a GOOD QUESTION!

How to Promote COGNITIVE RIGOR Through Classroom Questioning

ERIK M. FRANCIS

ASCD

Alexandria, Virginia USA

1703 N. Beauregard St. • Alexandria, VA 22311-1714 USA
Phone: 800-933-2723 or 703-578-9600 • Fax: 703-575-5400
Website: www.ascd.org • E-mail: member@ascd.org
Author guidelines: www.ascd.org/write

Deborah S. Delisle, *Executive Director;* Robert D. Clouse, *Managing Director, Digital Content & Publications;* Stefani Roth, *Publisher;* Genny Ostertag, *Director, Content Acquisitions;* Allison Scott, *Acquisitions Editor;* Julie Houtz, *Director, Book Editing & Production;* Georgia Park, *Senior Graphic Designer;* Mike Kalyan, *Manager, Production Services;* Valerie Younkin, *Production Designer;* Andrea Wilson, *Senior Production Specialist*

PAPERBACK ISBN: 978-1-4166-2075-4   ASCD product #116004   n07/16

PDF E-BOOK ISBN: 978-1-4166-2077-8; see Books in Print for other formats.

Quantity discounts: 10–49, 10%; 50+, 15%; 1,000+, special discounts (e-mail programteam@ascd.org or call 800-933-2723, ext. 5773, or 703-575-5773). For desk copies, go to www.ascd.org/deskcopy.

Library of Congress Cataloging-in-Publication Data
Names: Francis, Erik M.
Title: Now that's a good question! : how to promote cognitive rigor through
    classroom questioning / Erik M. Francis.
Description: Alexandria, Virginia : ASCD, [2016] | Includes bibliographical
    references and index.
Identifiers: LCCN 2016015250 (print) | LCCN 2016022889 (ebook) | ISBN
    9781416620754 (pbk. : alk. paper) | ISBN 9781416620778 (PDF)
Subjects: LCSH: Questioning. | Critical thinking--Study and teaching. |
    Learning, Psychology of. | Cognitive learning.
Classification: LCC LB1027.44 .F72 2016 (print) | LCC LB1027.44 (ebook) | DDC
    371.3/7--dc23
LC record available at https://lccn.loc.gov/2016015250

~ ~ ~

For my father, Frederick Lee Francis, and for my family

~ ~ ~

Now That's a Good Question!

Acknowledgments

There are many people to whom I am grateful for guidance and support not only in writing this book but also in helping me be where I am in my life, personally and professionally.

First, thank you to my family for their continuous encouragement and love not only through the process of writing this book but also through all the ups and downs; achievements and disappointments; risks and rewards; and setbacks, struggles, and success they experienced with me in my career: my wife Susie; my daughters Amanda, Madison, and Avery; my mom Julia Francis; my aunt and godmother Cookie Kalt; my mother Wendy Latman and her husband Wes Ervin; my sister Taylor; and my brothers Brett, Will, and Matt.

Thank you to my very good friends Michael Brien Lane, Monica Milinovich, Gary Horowitz, and Don Dolin for their loyalty and support, for always listening, and for always allowing me to bounce around ideas and thoughts with them.

Thank you to Jaime A. Castellano for my first opportunity to provide professional development to a school district and for my first opportunity to be published with the chapter we cowrote in his book *Talent Development for English Language Learners.*

Thank you to Karin Hess, John Walkup, and Ben Jones for coming up with the concept of cognitive rigor, for including me in the conversations about how to promote teaching for higher-order thinking and depth of knowledge, and for being colleagues.

Thank you to Allison Scott, my acquisitions editor at ASCD, for believing in this book from day one, for championing and shepherding it throughout the entire writing process, and, most especially, for helping fulfill my childhood dream of becoming a writer.

Thank you to Adrienne Gibson, Anthony Capuano, Linda Ihnat, and Nancy Konitzer for being mentors and guiding me to become the educator I am today. Also thanks to the colleagues with whom I have had the pleasure of working with and learning from in my professional endeavors—especially to Jean Read, Chris Kellen, Jay Parizek, Carol Bailin, Bobbie Orlando, Gary Fortney, Leeann Gilbreath, and Mark McManus.

Thank you to the schools, leaders, and educators with whom I have worked over the years—especially to Rhonda Newton, Eileen Frazier, and the staff at All Aboard Charter School in Phoenix, AZ; Adrian and Arlahee Ruiz, Adam Sharp, and the staff at Espiritu Community Development Corporation in Phoenix, AZ; Leanne Bowley of Phoenix Advantage Charter School in Phoenix, AZ; Sandy Breece and Padmaja Chava of Telesis Center for Learning in Lake Havasu, AZ; Melissa Yapo from Agua Fria Union School District in Avondale, AZ; Kelly Stewart and Anna Carino from Avondale Elementary District in Avondale, AZ; Heidi Manoguerra, Tyra Russell, and the staff at The Academy Charter School in Hempstead, NY; Sharon Hooker and the gifted education teachers from Sunnyside Unified School District in Sunnyside, AZ; Ron Alexander and Kim Steele from PLC Charter Schools in Tolleson, AZ; Sherry Ruttinger of Imagine Schools Arizona and Frank Stirpe of Imagine Prep at Superstition in Apache Junction, AZ; Jose Gonzalez and the staff of Planada Elementary District in Planada, CA; Brent Hanchey of Enterprise City Schools in Enterprise, AL; and Deltonya Warren, Nancy Edwards, and the core academic team of Eufaula City Schools in Eufaula City, AL (who helped come up with the "show and tell" method of rephrasing performance objectives of academic standards into good questions).

Finally, thank you to Frederick L. Francis, my father, my best friend, and my hero, who inspired my interest in teaching and learning, as well as my drive to succeed, and who also taught me the best question to prompt and encourage people to demonstrate and communicate their thinking: *What do you mean?*

Introduction:
What Does a Good Question Do?

You are teaching a lesson on identifying arithmetic patterns and how to explain them using the properties of operations. You present your students with the following math equations:

$$2 \times 2 =$$
$$3 \times 3 =$$
$$4 \times 4 =$$
$$5 \times 5 =$$
$$6 \times 6 =$$
$$7 \times 7 =$$
$$8 \times 8 =$$
$$9 \times 9 =$$

As your students prepare to solve the problems, you surprise them by presenting this material:

$$2 \times 2 = 2 + 2$$
$$3 \times 3 = 3 + 3 + 3$$
$$4 \times 4 = 4 + 4 + 4 + 4$$
$$5 \times 5 = 5 + 5 + 5 + 5 + 5$$
$$6 \times 6 = 6 + 6 + 6 + 6 + 6 + 6$$
$$7 \times 7 = 7 + 7 + 7 + 7 + 7 + 7 + 7$$
$$8 \times 8 = 8 + 8 + 8 + 8 + 8 + 8 + 8 + 8$$
$$9 \times 9 = 9 + 9 + 9 + 9 + 9 + 9 + 9 + 9 + 9$$

You then ask your students to respond to the questions in Figure 1.

Figure 1   The Cognitive Rigor Question (CRQ) Framework: Multiplication

ESSENTIAL	Universal	How can amount be determined?
	Overarching	How does mathematics involve abstract and quantitative reasoning?
	Topical	How can problems involving multiplication be represented and solved?
	Driving	How could you solve word problems using the following to represent the multiplication problem? • Drawings • Equations • A symbol representing the unknown number in the problem
FACTUAL		What is multiplication? What is the multiplier? What is the multiplicand? What is the product? What is a factor or coefficient?
ANALYTICAL		How can the products of whole numbers be interpreted? How can the unknown factor or product in a multiplication problem be determined given the following? • One factor and the product • Both factors (the multiplier and the multiplicand)
REFLECTIVE		What is the connection between addition and multiplication? What impact does the multiplier have on the multiplicand and the product?
HYPOTHETICAL		What if the multiplier in the given example problems were one more or one less? How could multiplication be used to solve problems involving the following? • Equal groups • Arrays • Measurement quantities
ARGUMENTATIVE		Is it easier to add or multiply?
AFFECTIVE		How could you interpret products of whole numbers in a certain context? How could you use multiplication within 100 to solve word problems? How could you determine the unknown product in a multiplication problem given the two factors (the multiplicand and multiplier)? How could you determine the unknown factor in a multiplication equation given one factor and the product?
PERSONAL		What do you want to learn about multiplication?

What are your students expected to do in this lesson—or rather, how deeply are they expected to communicate their learning? Clearly, you've asked students to "do the math," but the second set of math problems challenges your students to think deeply and to share their perspectives on how and why multiplication can be used to answer questions. That's the transferable knowledge we want them to learn so they can solve any multiplication problem they encounter.

So how might your students address the problems you've posed using the questions in Figure 1? The following are some potential outcomes. The students might:

• Say that multiplication is just "repeated addition" and explain how this process works using the examples you've provided.

• Demonstrate how whole numbers can be interpreted by explaining that 2 × 2 is actually the number of times that the number 2 is added to itself to attain the product of 4.

• Explain that the product of 3 × 3 is equivalent to adding 3 to itself three times. A visual solution might be to imagine adding up the total number of blocks in three block sets with each block set containing three separate blocks.

• Draw three sets of circles in three different places on a piece of paper and add them to get the correct result.

Any of these approaches fit this book's definition of the learning outcomes made possible by good questions. That's because good questions challenge students to do the following:

• **Read and research** texts and topics to build background knowledge.

• **Examine, experiment with, and explain** how and why concepts and procedures can be used in a variety of contexts.

• **Investigate and inquire** about what else needs to be known, could be done, or should be considered.

• **Design to demonstrate, develop, and differentiate talent and thinking** by showing what *you* can do with what *you* have learned.

These are the essential skills our students must learn. They also mark and measure what it truly means for a student to be college- and career-ready, including the ability to process their education and experience into expertise that they can transfer and use to address and respond to questions, problems, tasks, texts, and topics. These essential skills are also what students need to use to demonstrate and communicate their ability to think deeply and share the depth and extent of their knowledge and understanding.

The performance objectives of academic standards do not directly address these essential skills. The performance objectives are generally subject-specific learning goals or targets that set the criteria for what students must *demonstrate* or *show* they know, understand, and can do by the end of a particular grade level. They do not necessarily set the expectations for students to *communicate* or *tell* the depth and extent of their learning unless they are directed to *define, describe, explain, state,* or *write.*

However, these objectives can be developed into open-ended, thought-provoking good questions that will challenge students to demonstrate and communicate their knowledge and thinking.

We cannot simply rely on the curriculum to help students develop deeper thinking and learn how to transfer knowledge. Each passage or problem is an example or opportunity for students to apply what they are learning, but answering the questions or accomplishing the tasks correctly does not indicate that students truly learned the concept or content as deeply as they should. The accomplishments may merely indicate the students understood that specific text or were able to solve that particular problem. They do not guarantee that the students' response will be as cognitively complex as the question. As Gall (1970) explains, "It is not always possible to know whether a student answered a particular question by using a high-level cognitive process, such as analysis or synthesis, or by using the relatively low-level process of knowledge recall" (p. 710).

The good questions that we ask our students will not come from the standards or the texts. They will come from teachers and from our students. The questions, problems, tasks, texts, and topics presented in our curriculum can serve as the textual evidence that students can use to support their responses to good questions.

When we ask our students good questions, our objective is not only to assess what they know or what they can do with what they have learned. It is also to explore how deeply they are able to respond to questions. As Dillon (1988) puts it, "Our proper interest is not in the production of the correct answer but in the answer the student produces" (p. 67).

The true purpose and promise of this book is not merely to provide a description of a good question for educators or a list of good questions to ask students. The objective of this book is to help the reader understand how to craft good questions that do the following:

• Stimulate students' deeper thinking.
• Deepen students' knowledge, understanding, and awareness.
• Expand students' knowledge and extend their thinking.

- Pique students' curiosity, imagination, interest, and wonder.
- Encourage students to share the depth of their learning.

This book guides educators to create good cognitively rigorous questions that meet the criteria found in both Bloom's Revised Taxonomy and Webb's Depth-of-Knowledge (Hess, Carlock, Jones, & Walkup, 2009a, 2009b). It also shows how to develop good questions by rephrasing the learning goals and performance objectives from the following college- and career-ready academic standards:

- Common Core State Standards (CCSS) for English Language Arts and Literacy. From ©2010 National Governors Association Center for Best Practices and Council of Chief State School Officers (NGACBP & CCSSO). All rights reserved.
- Common Core State Standards (CCSS) for Mathematics. From ©2010 National Governors Association Center for Best Practices and Council of Chief State School Officers (NGACBP & CCSSO). All rights reserved.
- Next Generation Science Standards (NGSS). From NGSS Lead States, 2013. *Next Generation Science Standards: For States, By States*. Washington, DC: The National Academies Press.
- National History Standards (NHS). From National Center for History in the Schools, University of California, Los Angeles. ©1996 Regents of the University of California.
- College, Career, and Civic Life (C3) Framework for Social Studies State Standards. From National Council for the Social Studies (NCSS), *The College, Career, and Civic Life (C3) Framework for Social Studies State Standards: Guidance for Enhancing the Rigor of K–12 Civics, Economics, Geography, and History* (Silver Spring, MD: NCSS, 2013).

Good questions serve as the formative and summative assessments that measure the extent of a student's learning and they set the instructional focus for an active, student-centered learning experience.

When reading this book, do not focus solely on identifying the definition of good questions or picking examples of good questions. Instead, consider how you will use the information to develop learning experiences that are driven by inquiry and aimed at encouraging students to think deeply and share their learning.

If your students are demonstrating and communicating—or showing and telling—the depth and extent of what they are learning, then you'll know you've asked a good question.

1

What Is Questioning for Cognitive Rigor?

You are teaching a unit on the themes of heroism and courage using different texts of literary fiction and nonfiction. Your students are expected to do the following:

- Analyze how and why individuals, events, or ideas develop and interact over the course of a text. (CCSS.ELA-LITERACY.CCRA.R.3)

- Interpret words and phrases as they are used in a text, including determining technical, connotative, and figurative meanings, and analyze how specific word choices shape meaning or tone. (CCSS.ELA-LITERACY.CCRA.R.4)

- Analyze how two or more texts address similar themes or topics in order to build knowledge or to compare the approaches the authors take. (CCSS.ELA-LITERACY. CCRA.R.9)

- Write informative/explanatory texts to examine and convey complex ideas and information clearly and accurately through the effective selection, organization, and analysis of content. (CCSS.ELA-LITERACY.CCRA.W.2)

- Draw evidence from literary or informational texts to support analysis, reflection, and research. (CCSS.ELA-LITERACY.CCRA.W.9)

Your students will address and respond to the good questions in Figure 1.1 during the unit.

Take a look at the questions that students will address as part of this literary genre study (set aside the figure's format for now). Notice how the questions engage students to do—or demonstrate—the following:

- **Recognize and understand** data, definitions, and details.
- **Apply** concepts and procedures.

Figure 1.1   Good Questions: Heroism

ESSENTIAL	**Universal**	What is heroism? What is courage? What makes someone heroic or courageous?
	Overarching	How do characters develop and interact over the course of a text? How can words and phrases be interpreted as they are used in a text, including determining technical, connotative, and figurative meanings? How do two or more texts address similar themes or topics in order to build knowledge or to compare the approaches the authors take? How do narratives use effective techniques, well-chosen details, and well-structured event sequences to develop real or imagined experiences? How can evidence from literary or informational texts be drawn to support analysis, reflection, and research?
	Topical	How do the heroes and acts of courage presented in literary fiction and nonfiction text reflect the beliefs, ideals, and values of different authors, cultures, eras, generations, and societies?
	Driving	How could you create a character who does the following? • Embodies the qualities and traits of a hero • Reflects your personal beliefs and traits of a hero • Represents your culture or generation's beliefs and ideas about heroism
FACTUAL		Who is the hero in a story? What are the character traits of a hero? What are the different types of heroes? Who is the hero in the texts read or reviewed as part of this unit? What is a "mirror character"? What words do the authors of these texts for this unit use to describe the hero in the story, the situation encountered, or the actions and deeds committed by the hero?
ANALYTICAL		What distinguishes a hero from the main character or protagonist in the story? What are the similarities and differences among different types of heroes? What distinguishes the hero from all other individuals in a text? What is the difference between a hero and an idol? How does the author characterize, describe, or portray the hero in the text? What is the tone of texts that express and share acts of heroism and courage? What does it mean when a hero "falls from grace"?

REFLECTIVE	What is the relationship between the hero and the villain? The hero and the literary foil?
	What influences do tales of heroes, heroism, and courage have on an audience?
	What influence does time, geography, and social factors have on the definitions and perceptions of a hero, heroism, or courage?
	What effect does the language the author uses have on how a hero or heroic act is presented or portrayed?
HYPOTHETICAL	How could a hero be tempted or "fall from grace"?
	What could turn a hero into a villain?
	How could a villain become a hero?
	How could the flaws of a character make the character more heroic?
	How could a hero and villain be "mirror characters"?
	How could a hero and the foil be "mirror characters"?
	What if the hero or villain was female and a male character was in peril?
ARGUMENTATIVE	Are the protagonist and antagonist of a story also the hero or villain, or do they have different meanings?
	Must a hero be perfect or can a hero be flawed?
	Must a hero be fearless in order to be heroic, or can fear help the hero become more heroic?
	Is there a universal understanding of what makes someone heroic or courageous, or does it depend upon certain factors (e.g., people, place, time)?
AFFECTIVE	What do you think it means to be a hero?
	What do you think makes someone heroic or courageous?
	Who is your hero and why?
	What is a heroic act committed by a real person or group of people that deserves to be acknowledged or recognized? How would you clearly and effectively share this act of heroism with an audience?
	Is the hero in the story you are reading a hero or an idol?
	Is the hero in the story you are writing a hero or an idol?
PERSONAL	What do you want to learn about heroism and courage and how they are portrayed in literary fiction and nonfiction?

- **Analyze and evaluate causes, connections, and consequences**—actual, hypothetical, or potential.
- **Think creatively** about what they personally can design, develop, or do with what they have learned.

Demonstrating thinking is half the battle. These questions also encourage students to communicate the following:

- **What is the knowledge** that must be read, researched, and recognized?
- **How can this knowledge be used** to answer questions, address problems, accomplish tasks, and analyze texts and topics?
- **Why can this knowledge be used** to study phenomena, solve problems, and solidify ideas?
- **How else could *you* use this knowledge** in different academic and real-world contexts?

These are the actions and conditions that define rigor—and in particular instructional rigor—that challenge students to learn concepts and retain content at higher and deeper levels (Blackburn, 2008). When we describe a learning experience as rigorous or having rigor, we are talking about its level of cognitive rigor—the extent to which students are challenged to demonstrate higher-order thinking and communicate depth of knowledge.

What Is Cognitive Rigor?

Cognitive rigor has received increased attention primarily due to instructional shifts in K–12 education that place importance on developing 21st century skills, which are generally agreed to be skills that prepare students for college and career success. As a result, greater expectations are now placed "on education systems around the world to teach in ways that produce the knowledge workers and innovators businesses need to compete in the 21st century knowledge economy" (Trilling & Fadel, 2009, p. 61). Students still need to acquire and apply knowledge accurately. However, they must also be able to analyze and articulate knowledge authentically through critical thinking and problem solving, collaboration and communication, and creativity and innovation.

Cognitive rigor measures the depth and breadth of topics that should be taught as part of an educational experience based on the following criteria:

- **Complexity of the concepts and content** taught and obtained
- **Kind of knowledge** acquired

- **Type of thinking** demonstrated
- **Depth of knowledge** communicated (Hess et al., 2009a, 2009b; Walkup & Jones, 2014)

Cognitive rigor provides this enhanced educational experience by superimposing two academic frameworks that define how deeply students demonstrate their knowledge—Bloom's Revised Taxonomy and Webb's Depth-of-Knowledge (Hess et al., 2009a, 2009b). Bloom's taxonomy categorizes the *kind of knowledge* and *type of thinking* that students demonstrate to answer a question. Webb's Depth-of-Knowledge model designates the *depth of knowledge* that students express in a given context to answer a question. By aligning these two frameworks, cognitive rigor acts as a high-quality instructional tool to ensure teachers prepare their students for success in and out of the classroom. (We'll discuss how these two frameworks work together to promote cognitive rigor in just a bit.)

Another important aspect of cognitive rigor is that it promotes *intellectual involvement* by challenging students to explain what they have learned in their own unique way. Students must learn how to become meaning-seeking critical thinkers who can sift through and process vast amounts of information and then use the deeper knowledge they gain in a variety of academic and real-world contexts. It is the job of educators to provide learning experiences that encourage such deep examination of knowledge. In this way, the use of cognitive rigor as a *measurement tool* supports the use of cognitive rigor as the comprehensive *learning goal* for students.

Later in this chapter, we will discuss how this learning goal promotes cognitive rigor through better classroom questioning (i.e., asking *good questions*). First let's take a look at how cognitive rigor fosters authentic teaching and deep learning experiences for teachers and their students. Refer to Figure 1.2.

Higher-Order Thinking

The revised version of Bloom's taxonomy developed by Anderson and Krathwohl (2001) models cognitive rigor by clearly differentiating knowledge (*What is to be learned?*) from thinking (*How is learning to be demonstrated?*) by splitting both into two dimensions. The Knowledge Dimension defines the *content or subject matter* students need to learn—the facts, the vocabulary, the concepts, the procedures, and the criteria for using all four. The Cognitive Process Dimension describes the *thinking or skills* students must develop and demonstrate. Anderson and Krathwohl's (2001) revised version rephrases these cognitive skills as verbs to help teachers develop learning goals and performance objectives, which is the intent and purpose of both the original taxonomy and its revised version. However, as formatted and presented, the taxonomy still remains limited as a resource for classifying and creating good questions.

To develop good questions with Bloom's Revised Taxonomy, we can use the basic categories from Bloom's Questioning Inverted Pyramid to replace the cognitive verbs of performance objectives with the following question stems:

Figure 1.2   Good Questions and Bloom's Taxonomy

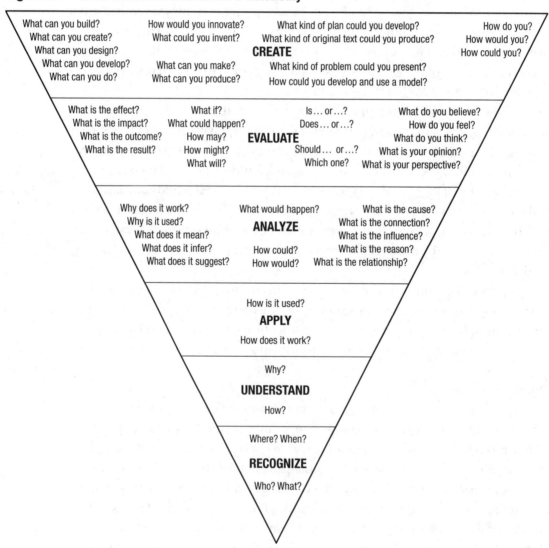

Source: Categories adapted from Anderson & Krathwohl, 2001

- **Recognize:** Who? What? Where? When?
- **Understand:** How? Why?
- **Apply:** How does it work? How is it used?
- **Analyze:** Why does it work? Why is it used? What does it imply/infer? What does it mean? What does it suggest? What is the cause? What is the connection? What is the influence? What is the reason? What is the relationship?
- **Evaluate:** What is the effect? What is the impact? What is the outcome? What is the result? What if? What would happen? What could happen? What do you believe about it? How do you feel about it? What do you think about it? What is your opinion about it?
- **Create:** What can you create? What can you design? What can you develop? What can you plan? What can you produce? How could you innovate? What could you invent? How do you? How could you? How would you? How could you develop and use a model? What kind of original text could you produce? What kind of problem could you present?

By replacing the cognitive verbs with the correlating question stems in Figure 1.2, students will be challenged to demonstrate—or show—and also to communicate—or tell—the depth of their knowledge and understanding. Figure 1.3 demonstrates how rephrasing questions creates more cognitively complex performance tasks.

The performance objectives in column 1 of Figure 1.3 provide explicit learning expectations. They also challenge students to demonstrate—or *show*—how deeply they can think about the texts and topics they are reading and reviewing in class. However, performance objectives are limited in engaging students to communicate—or *tell*—the depth and extent of their understanding, which is a key component of teaching and learning for cognitive rigor. With good questions such as the ones posed in column 2, students are prompted to think deeply and share the depth of their learning by explaining *how and why the answer is correct.*

Depth of Knowledge

Depth of knowledge designates the context in which students will demonstrate and communicate their learning. The context is situational and depends upon the extent the text, the topic, or even the teacher expects the student to demonstrate and communicate learning. Is the student expected to develop deep knowledge and understanding of the text or topic being read and reviewed? Is the student expected to demonstrate and communicate how or why the concepts and content can be used to attain and explain answers, outcomes, and results? Is the student expected

Figure 1.3   Good Questions and Learning Objectives

LEARNING OBJECTIVES	GOOD QUESTION
Compare and contrast stories in the same genre (e.g., mysteries or adventures) on their approaches to similar themes and topics.	How are stories in the same genre similar and different in how they address and approach similar themes and topics?
Determine the central idea and themes addressed in the novel *The Outsiders*.	How does *The Outsiders* address the following themes: stereotyping, wealth and poverty, honor and loyalty, friendship and family, book smart vs. street smart, school vs. experience?
Analyze the role of women in *Romeo and Juliet* and how that affects the development of the plot and characters.	What role do women play in *Romeo and Juliet* and how does that affect the development of plot and characters?
Solve these equations. $9 \times 2 = \quad 5 \times 6 = \quad 7 \times 3 = \quad 4 \times 6 = \quad 10 \times 8 =$	How can multiplication be used to solve these equations? $9 \times 2 = \quad 5 \times 6 = \quad 7 \times 3 = \quad 4 \times 6 = \quad 10 \times 8 =$
Use the four operations to solve word problems involving distances, intervals of time, liquid volumes, masses of objects, and money, including problems involving simple fractions or decimals, and problems that require expressing measurements given in a larger unit in terms of a smaller unit.	How can the four operations be used to solve word problems involving the following? • Distance • Intervals of time • Liquid volumes • Masses of objects • Money • Simple fractions or decimals • Converting smaller or larger measurements
List 5 ways energy can be conserved in the home.	How can energy be conserved in the home?
In its orbit around the sun, Mars is 154,900,000 miles at its most distant point. Express this distance in scientific notation.	How can the mileage of Mars be expressed in scientific notation at its most distant point from the sun?
Explain what turgor pressure is and why it is important to plants.	What is turgor pressure and why is it important to plants?
Compare and contrast family life historically and presently among various cultures. Consider such things as communication, technology, homes, transportation, recreation, schools, and cultural traditions.	How has family life among various cultures changed or remained the same (historically and presently) in regard to • Communication • Technology • Homes • Transportation • Recreation • School • Cultural traditions
Understand that the U.S. government was formed by British colonists who fought for independence from England.	How was the U.S. government established by British colonists who fought for independence from England?
Debate whether President Truman was justified for dropping the atomic bomb on Japan.	Was President Truman justified, unjustified, or did he have no other option but to drop the atomic bomb on Japan?

to transfer and use the concepts and content to address academic and real-world ideas and issues across the curriculum and beyond the classroom? When we refer to depth of knowledge, we're determining not only *how much* a student knows but also *how extensively* he understands and is aware of the concepts and content he is learning.

Teaching and learning for cognitive rigor uses the Depth-of-Knowledge (DOK) model designed by Norman Webb (1997, 2002) to designate *how extensively* students communicate their knowledge and understanding of concepts and content. This model, shown also in Figure 1.4, consists of four levels:

• **DOK Level 1 (Recall and Reproduction):** Students describe *what knowledge* needs to be acquired and developed in order to think deeply about texts and topics.

• **DOK Level 2 (Application of Skills and Concepts):** Students convey *how the knowledge can be used* to answer questions, address problems, or accomplish tasks or analyze texts and topics.

• **DOK Level 3 (Strategic Thinking and Reasoning):** Students examine and explain *why the knowledge can be used* to defend and support responses and results.

• **DOK Level 4 (Extended Thinking):** Students study and share *what or how else the knowledge can be used* in a variety of academic and real-world circumstances.

The categories in Bloom's taxonomy define the *subject matter* and describe the *skills* students must learn, whereas the levels of Webb's DOK model designate the scenario, setting, or situation in which students demonstrate and communicate their learning. Webb's levels do not scaffold in their complexity but indicate four different ways that students share the depth and extent of their learning. Hess (2013) describes the DOK levels as ceilings that designate how deeply students are expected to explain and use what they learn. Therefore, a higher DOK level does not necessarily mean it is "better" or even more desirable than other levels. It just provides a deeper context for the transfer and use of student learning. Consider how the following scenario engages students to share the depth of their understanding of the Pythagorean Theorem and its converse.

You are teaching a unit on the Pythagorean Theorem. Your students are expected to do the following:

• Explain a proof of the Pythagorean Theorem and its converse. (CCSS.MATH. CONTENT.8.G.B.6)

- Apply the Pythagorean Theorem to determine unknown side lengths in right triangles in real-world and mathematical problems in two and three dimensions. (CCSS.MATH.CONTENT.8.G.B.7)

- Apply the Pythagorean Theorem to find the distance between two points in a coordinate system. (CCSS.MATH.CONTENT.8.G.B.8)

Your students will respond to the good questions in Figure 1.5.

Figure I.4   Good Questions and Depth of Knowledge

What is the knowledge?	How can the knowledge be used?	Why can the knowledge be used?	What else can be done with the knowledge?
DOK-1	DOK-2	DOK-3	DOK-4
RECALL AND REPRODUCTION	BASIC APPLICATION OF SKILLS AND CONCEPTS	STRATEGIC THINKING	EXTENDED THINKING
Who?	How does it happen?	Why does it work?	What is the impact?
What?	How does it work?	Why is it the answer?	What is the influence?
Where?	How is it used?	Why is it the outcome?	What if?
When?	What is the answer?	Why is it the result?	What would happen?
How?	What is the outcome?	What does it infer?	What could happen?
Why?	What is the result?	What does it suggest?	What will?
	What can you do?	What is the cause/effect?	What else?
	How can you use it?	What distinguishes/indicates?	How else?
	How would you use it?	What is the reason?	What do you believe/feel/think?
		What is the relationship?	What can you build/create/design/develop/produce?
		How could you develop and use a model?	What kind of plan could you develop?
		How could you?	What kind of text could you write?
			What kind of problem could you present?

Source: Framework adapted from Webb 1997, 2002; Hess 2009a, 2009b

Figure I.5   Good Questions and The Pythagorean Theorem

ESSENTIAL	**Universal**	How can objects in life be categorized, classified, defined, described, determined, and quantified?
	Overarching	How can mathematics be used to solve problems in everyday life, society, and the workplace? How can the characteristics and properties of two- and three-dimensional geometric shapes be analyzed? How can mathematical arguments about geometric relationship be developed?
	Topical	How and why can the Pythagorean Theorem be used to address and solve problems involving right triangles?
	Driving	How can you explain a proof of the Pythagorean Theorem and its converse? What kind of mathematical or real-world problem could you design that would require using the Pythagorean Theorem or its converse?
FACTUAL		What is a right triangle? What is the Pythagorean Theorem? What is the converse of the Pythagorean Theorem? What do the lettered sides of the triangle represent? What is the hypotenuse of a right triangle? What is a coordinate plane?
ANALYTICAL		How can the Pythagorean Theorem be applied to determine unknown side lengths in right triangles in real-world and mathematical problems in two and three dimensions? How can the Pythagorean Theorem be applied to find the distance between two points on the coordinate plane?
REFLECTIVE		What is the relationship between the length of sides, the length of the hypotenuse, and the angles of the triangle according to the Pythagorean Theorem? What effect does the length of the sides and hypotenuse of a triangle have on the angles of the triangle and the type of triangle a shape is?
HYPOTHETICAL		What if the length of the hypotenuse is given but the length of one of the sides is not? How could the following individuals use the Pythagorean Theorem in the following situations? • A firefighter needs to determine where to position the ladder on a fire truck to put out a fire and save lives in a burning building. • A baseball player wants to determine where to hit the ball so the infielders cannot catch it in the air or intercept it as a groundball. • A tennis player must determine where to serve a ball. • Katniss Everdeen from *The Hunger Games* must determine how far to shoot her arrow from her position in a tree at the tributes standing on the ground below her.
ARGUMENTATIVE		• Should the numerical value that is determined to be the length of the hypotenuse be rounded to the nearest whole number or should it be expressed in its complete or true form? • Should Pythagoras be credited for founding the theorem or should other civilizations predating Pythagoras be credited?

(continued)

Figure 1.5   Good Questions and The Pythagorean Theorem (*continued*)

AFFECTIVE	How would you use the Pythagorean Theorem in the following situations? • Design a project for art class. • Decide how high to extend a ladder to paint the side of a house. • Determine the dimensions of a television, a suitcase, or a computer. • Determine the distance between three points on a map. • Determine how far a quarterback threw a football to one of his receivers. How could you use the Pythagorean Theorem and its converse to determine what kind of triangle is presented in a given problem?
PERSONAL	What do you want to learn about the Pythagorean Theorem and its converse?

Notice how the levels of thinking scaffold progressively, moving from basic levels (recognizing, understanding, and applying) to more complex levels of demonstrating learning (analyzing, evaluating). However, the depth to which students express their learning depends upon the context. Some questions focus specifically on reciting and reproducing specific knowledge about the Pythagorean Theorem and its converse (DOK-1). Some questions ask students to explain *how the Pythagorean Theorem can be used* (DOK-2) or *why the theorem can be used* (DOK-3) to attain and explain answers and solutions. Some questions ask students to share *what else could be done with the Pythagorean theorem and its converse* or *how else could the Pythagorean Theorem be used* (DOK-4) in different academic and real-world situations. Although the level of thinking is progressive, the depth of knowledge is more extensive.

When teaching and learning for cognitive rigor, keep in mind that depth of knowledge is not the same as higher-order thinking. Higher-order thinking defines the action or cognition (thinking). Depth of knowledge designates the context or scope in which the cognitive action is performed. Together, higher-order thinking and depth of knowledge promote cognitive rigor by setting the instructional expectations for *how deeply and extensively* students will demonstrate and communicate—or show and tell—what they have learned.

How Can We Promote Cognitive Rigor by Asking Good Questions?

Teaching and learning for cognitive rigor is very different from teaching and learning in traditional educational settings that are driven solely by objectives and outcomes. Cognitive rigor prompts and encourages students to think deeply and to express and share the depth of their learning by addressing and responding to good questions that serve as formative and summative assessments and set the instructional focus for learning.

It's an approach that can be applied to both the setting of educational objectives and the development of good questions using the following formula:

Show and tell + HOT Question Stem + DOK Context

The HOT Question Stem correlates to a specific cognitive category of Bloom's Questioning Inverted Pyramid (see the categories in Figure 1.2, p. 12). For example, when a performance objective challenges a student *to understand*, or one of its correlating verbs in its cognitive category in Bloom's Revised Taxonomy, we can replace the verb with the question stems *how* or *why*. These two question stems prompt students to demonstrate and communicate their understanding and encourage them to think strategically (DOK-3) and extend their thinking (DOK-4) beyond the subject matter and situation originally presented in the performance objective—and that's exactly what we want. When converting performance objectives to good questions that promote cognitive rigor, you may find yourself using the question stem *how* or *why* often—and that's OK. Challenge yourself, however, to use the other question stems listed within Figure 1.2.

The DOK context addresses both the scope of a learning activity as well as the expected depth of content understanding (Hess et al., 2009a, 2009b). This is typically defined by the noun phrase that follows the verb of a performance objective. It not only establishes the scope of the activity but also sets expectations for how deeply students demonstrate their learning.

Notice how the good questions in Figure 1.6 are derived from performance objectives. The verb of the performance objective is replaced with the appropriate question stem that prompts students *to think*. The noun phrase following the verb of the performance objective designates the context or depth students must use to explain their learning. These good questions set the instructional focus and serve as formative and summative assessments of a lesson or unit. (We'll discuss how to convert performance objectives into good questions at the end of this chapter.)

How Can We Teach with Cognitive Rigor Questions?

Each type of cognitive rigor question guides students to pursue deeper knowledge and respond insightfully to the questions in their own unique way. These questions also allow teachers to act as both the instructor who provides the information students must learn and the facilitator who encourages students to process information into expertise or other knowledge outcomes (including self-knowledge).

Figure 1.6   Making Good Standards-Based Questions

LEARNING OBJECTIVE	STARTER STATEMENT	HOT STEM	DOK CONTEXT
Distinguish long from short vowel sounds in spoken single-syllable words.	Show and tell	what distinguishes	long from short vowel sounds in spoken single-syllable words?
Determine central ideas or themes of a text and analyze their development; summarize the key supporting details and ideas.	Show and tell	how	• can the central ideas and themes of text be determined? • do the central ideas and themes develop over the course of a text? • do the key supporting details and ideas support the central ideas and themes of a text?

Analyze how two or more authors writing about the same topic shape their presentations of key information by emphasizing different evidence or advancing different interpretations of facts.	Show and tell	how could	• two or more authors writing about the same topic shape their presentations of key information by doing the following?
			  - emphasizing different evidence
			  - advancing different interpretations of facts

Write arguments to support claims in an analysis of substantive topics or texts using valid reasoning and relevant and sufficient evidence.	Show and tell	how could you	write an argument that supports claims in an analysis of substantive topics or texts using valid reasoning and relevant and sufficient evidence?
Determine or clarify the meaning of unknown and multiple-meaning words and phrases by using context clues, analyzing meaningful word parts, and consulting general and specialized reference materials, as appropriate.	Show and tell	what is the reason	the meaning of unknown and multiple-meaning words can be determined and clarified using the following? • context clues • meaningful word part • consulting general and specialized reference materials
Count to 120, starting at any number less than 120. In this range, read and write numerals and represent a number of objects with a written numeral.	Show and tell	how could you	• count to 120, starting at a number less than 120? • read and write numerals? • represent a number of objects with a written numeral?
Multiply one-digit whole numbers by multiples of 10 in the range 10–90 (e.g., 9×80, 5×60) using strategies based on place value and properties of operations.	Show and tell	how could you	multiply one-digit whole numbers by multiples of 10 in the range from 10 to 90 using strategies based upon the following? • place value • the properties of operations

Understand that a function from one set (called the domain) to another set (called the range) assigns to each element of the domain exactly one element of the range. If f is a function and x is an element of its domain, then $f(x)$ denotes the output of f corresponding to the input x. The graph of f is the graph of the equation $y = f(x)$.	Show and tell	how	• does a function from one set (called the domain) to another set (called the range) assigns to each element of the domain exactly one element of the range? • does $f(x)$ denote the output of f corresponding to the input x if f is a function and x is an element of its domain? • is the graph of f the graph of the equation $y = f(x)$?

• **Essential questions** set the instructional focus and expectations for students to demonstrate deeper, more authentic learning about universal themes, core ideas, and topical understandings of a lesson or unit in their own unique way.

• **Factual questions** direct students to read, research, and recognize information about *who, what, where,* or *when.*

• **Analytical questions** challenge students to examine and explain *how* and *why, what is the meaning* or *message, what is the intent* or *purpose, what categorizes* or *characterizes, what determines* or *indicates, what are the similarities and differences,* and *what is inferred, represented, signified, suggested,* or *symbolized.*

• **Reflective questions** engage students to investigate and inquire *what are the cause and effects, impact and influences, reasons and results,* and *advantages and disadvantages.*

• **Hypothetical questions** prompt students to imagine *what if,* hypothesize *what would happen, what could happen, how may,* and *how might,* and predict *what will* or *how will.*

• **Argumentative questions** involve students in *making choices* and *defending decisions* supported with valid reasoning and relevant and sufficient evidence.

• **Affective questions** encourage students to share *what do* you *believe, feel,* or *think;* state *what is* your *opinion, perspective,* or *thoughts;* or show *how could* you or *how would* you address a particular issue, problem, or situation.

• **Personal questions** motivate students to take the initiative to explore *what do you want to learn* about the subjects and topics being taught and then share their learning with their classmates.

These cognitive rigor questions (CRQs) can serve as the essential question for a single lesson or even an entire unit. They can also be grouped together using the CRQ Framework (see Appendix A). Clearly all these questions cannot be answered within a single class period since there are just too many of them! However, each question can be asked individually or paired with other questions to provide a deeper, student-centered learning experience that promotes cognitive rigor.

Conclusion

Questioning for cognitive rigor engages students to demonstrate and communicate the deep knowledge and complex thinking skills they can use in both their academic studies and in their personal lives. We can create these good questions simply by rephrasing academic standards and their performance objectives into open-ended, thought-provoking inquiries or devise our own questions to set the instructional focus and serve as assessments for student learning. The CRQ Framework can be used as a resource that not only identifies the kind of questions to ask but also scaffolds questions based upon their intent, purpose, and level of complexity.

The rest of this book explores each question category within this CRQ Framework and shows how each category builds on the others to increase the level of thinking and depth of knowledge—or cognitive rigor—students are expected to demonstrate. We will also address how students respond to these questions and how teachers can assess the accuracy, acceptability, appropriateness, and authenticity of their responses.

PROFESSIONAL DEVELOPMENT

How to Develop Good Questions from Learning Objectives

Objective

Develop cognitive rigor questions derived from the performance objectives of college- and career-ready standards that will serve as the instructional focus and formative/summative assessment of a lesson or unit.

Materials

- College- and career-ready standards adopted by your state
- Curriculum and texts adopted by your school
- Good Questions and Bloom's Taxonomy (Figure 1.2)
- Good Questions and Depth of Knowledge (Figure 1.4)

Procedure

    1. Select the standards that will be addressed as part of the lesson or unit. Using Figure 1.7, insert that performance objective under the column called Learning Objectives.

    2. Replace the cognitive verb at the beginning of the performance objective with its correlating HOT Question Stem from the Bloom's Questioning Inverted Pyramid. Place the stem under the column headed by HOT Stem.

    3. Identify the subject matter or knowledge that will be learned and the scenario, setting, or situation in which the subject matter will be addressed and used. Place those terms in the column labeled DOK Context. See Figure 1.6 for examples.

    4. Rephrase the noun phrase at the end of the performance objective of the standard. Write the phrase next to the HOT Stem converted from the cognitive verb.

    5. Combine the HOT Stem with the DOK Context to form your cognitive rigor question. This will be the good question that sets the instructional focus and serves as the formative and summative assessment for the lesson or unit. See Figure 1.6 for an example of a completed chart.

Figure 1.7   Creating Good Questions from Learning Objectives

LEARNING OBJECTIVES	STARTER STATEMENT	HOT STEM	DOK CONTEXT
	Show and tell		
	Show and tell		
	Show and tell		
	Show and tell		

2

What Makes a Good Question Essential?

You are teaching a unit on the 1950s and 1960s civil rights movement. Your students are expected to do the following:

- The student understands the "Second Reconstruction" and its advancement of civil rights. (NHS.USE9.4.A.)

- Create and use a chronological sequence of related events to compare developments that happened at the same time and analyze and evaluate how historical events and developments were shaped by unique circumstances of time and place as well as broader historical contexts. (C3.D2.His.1)

- Compare life in specific historical time periods to life today and analyze change and continuity in historical eras by classifying series of historical events and developments as examples (C3.D2.His.2)

- Compare perspectives of people in the past to those of people in the present and explain and analyze how and why complex and interacting factors influenced the perspectives of people during different historical eras. (C3.D2.His.4)

- Explain and analyze how and why historical contexts shaped and continue to shape people's perspectives. (C3.D2.His.5)

Your students will respond to the good questions outlined in Figure 2.1.

Take a look at the good questions that have been determined to be essential for this unit on the civil rights movement. Note how the universal questions in Figure 2.1 focus on broad ideas and themes and the overarching questions encourage students to examine the historical and social context of ideas and events. These questions help students build thinking skills and develop broader awareness of the ideas and issues and deep conceptual understanding of academic subjects. The question in the topical category *How were civil rights addressed and advanced during*

Figure 2.1   Good Essential Questions: Civil Rights

ESSENTIAL	Universal	What is social justice? What are civil rights? What are a person's rights and how are they determined? How should someone advocate or "fight" for their rights? How can one person make a difference? Should equality require government action or is it a natural right?
	Overarching	How can a chronological sequence of historically related events be created and used to compare events across a time continuum? How were specific historical events shaped by unique circumstances of time and place as well as the broader historical contexts? What distinguishes specific historical time periods from life today? What distinguishes perspectives of people in the past to those of people in the present? How and why have interacting factors influenced the perspectives of people during different historical eras? How can change during historical eras be analyzed by classifying a series of historical events and/or developments as examples? How and why do historical contexts shape people's perspectives today?
	Topical	How were civil rights addressed and advanced during the Second Reconstruction of the 1950s and 1960s?
	Driving	How could *you* create a chronological document that details and explains the following: • The incidents and outcomes of the civil rights movement • The ways these events were shaped by the unique time and place circumstances of the Second Reconstruction • The impact and influence these events had on later civil rights issues

the Second Reconstruction of the 1950s and 1960s? describes how deeply students are expected to demonstrate their learning. The final driving question prompts students and engages students to create a chronological document that details the events of the Second Reconstruction and illustrates the causes and effect on history and society. These good questions are the vital—or essential—questions that set the instructional focus and serve as the summative assessment for student learning.

What Good Essential Questions Do

Good essential questions focus on crucial ideas and key understandings. The CRQ Framework identifies four subcategories of essential questions associated with the learning experience:

• **Universal questions** that address grander, more global ideas, issues, themes, or topics.

• **Overarching questions** that focus on the core ideas of an academic discipline.

• **Topical questions** that identify the central understandings of a lesson or unit.

• **Driving questions** that prompt students to share the depth of their learning in their own way.

Consider the examples of these subcategories of essential questions in Figure 2.2.

Figure 2.2   The Four Types of Good Essential Questions

ESSENTIAL	**Universal**	What are the global ideas, issues, or themes being addressed?
	Overarching	What are the core ideas and key understandings presented in the academic material?
	Topical	What is the instructional focus and summative assessment of the lesson?
	Driving	What can *you* create, design, develop, do, plan, or produce that reflects the depth of *your* learning?

Separately, these subcategories focus on what Wiggins and McTighe (2005) identify as "four different but overlapping meanings for the term *essential* when used to characterize questions" (pp.108–109). Together, these essential questions provide the basis for a meaningful learning experience that promotes cognitive rigor. Let's take a look at how each type of essential question establishes instructional focus and serves as the summative assessment for a lesson or even an entire course of study.

Universal Essential Questions

Good universal questions engage students to reflect upon the ethical, philosophical, and existential concerns unearthed by topics, no matter the academic discipline. Wiggins and McTighe (2005) describe such questions as "the important questions that recur throughout all our lives—broad in scope… timeless in nature… perpetually arguable… [and] invariably provisional" (p.108). As such, these questions set the stage for future deep thinking capability. These questions should not be used for assessment or evaluation but rather as prompts for discussion that encourage students to think deeply about their own (and their classmates') opinions and perceptions.

Consider the question *What is death?* How would a scientist, a religious leader, a lawyer, an author, or an artist respond to this question? How do the legal, scientific, and religious definitions of death differ? Students tackling such difficult questions increase their self-awareness capabilities and build a keener understanding of the wider world they inhabit. Good questions drive home the point that there is more than one way to consider a question. As Wiggins and McTighe (2005) note, "education is not just about learning 'the answer' but learning how to learn" (p. 108).

Universal questions can be helpful when teaching students how to determine the central idea or theme of texts. Universal questions prompt students to think deeply about those universal ideas and issues addressed or alluded to in a literary or informational text. The topical essential question then challenges students to think critically about how the text addresses that particular theme and how to cite specific evidence from the text that supports their response. For example, suppose the topical essential question asks students to show and tell *How does* The Giver *by Lois Lowry address the themes of isolation, the value of memory, choices, pleasure and pain, old age, and conformity versus individuality?* These themes can be examined and explored more deeply by asking students to consider and comment on *what does isolation mean, what is the value of memory, what impacts and influences our choices, what distinguishes pleasure and pain, what is old age,* and *what is the difference between conformity and individuality.* These universal questions will broaden students' awareness of these grander ideas and issues and provide students with a better understanding of how the text they are reading and reviewing infers or references these themes and topics. Later in this chapter, see Figure 2.5 (p. 31) for an example of how universal and topical essential questions can be used to teach themes with *Charlotte's Web* by E. B. White. You can also find examples of good universal questions in Appendix B.

Overarching Essential Questions

Good overarching questions address "the core inquiries within an academic discipline" (Wiggins & McTighe, 2005, p. 109). Such questions support the development of disciplinary literacy by "[emphasizing] the specialized knowledge and abilities possessed by those who create, communicate, and use knowledge within each of the disciplines" (Shanahan & Shanahan, 2012, p. 7). Good overarching questions address these disciplinary core ideas by focusing on

- The "big ideas" that establish the purpose of an academic discipline.
- The enduring understandings of an accepted or proven academic area.
- The technical knowledge resident in an academic field of study.

These important ideas and core processes are central to an academic discipline and extend beyond the classroom. They mark and measure what it means to be literate and skilled in a particular area, subject, or field of study. Ideally, students should continuously address and revisit overarching questions such as these throughout their entire academic careers. Figure 2.3 provides examples of good overarching questions that address the core ideas of different academic disciplines.

Appendix C shows how the performance objectives of college and career anchor standards can be converted into good overarching questions that address the disciplinary core ideas of academic subjects. These essential questions are appropriate to ask at any grade level and can serve as subject-area benchmark and summative assessments.

Topical Essential Questions

Good topical questions set the instructional expectations for learning and focus on the grade-level or course-specific standards. Consider the following scenario for teaching the number system, expressions, and equations at the 8th grade level.

You are teaching a unit on rational numbers. Your students are expected to do the following:

- Know that numbers that are not rational are called irrational. Understand informally that every number has a decimal expansion; for rational numbers show that the decimal expansion repeats eventually, and convert a decimal expansion which repeats eventually into a rational number. (CCSS.MATH.CONTENT.8.NS.A.1)

- Use rational approximations of irrational numbers to compare the size of irrational numbers, locate them approximately on a number line diagram, and estimate the value of expressions (e.g., π^2). (CCSS.MATH.CONTENT.8.NS.A.2)

- Use square root and cube root symbols to represent solutions to equations of the form $x^2 = p$ and $x^3 = p$, where p is a positive rational number. Evaluate square roots of small perfect squares and cube roots of small perfect cubes. Know that $\sqrt{2}$ is irrational. (CCSS.MATH.CONTENT.8.EE.A.2)

Your students will respond to the questions in Figure 2.4.

Figure 2.3   Good Overarching Questions Across the Content Areas

TEXTUAL LITERACY	• What is the relationship between reading, writing, speaking, listening, and grammar and vocabulary? • How can ideas and information be expressed using oral, written, creative, or technical expression? • How do texts and authors express perspectives through writing style, vocabulary, language, or how the work is produced?
MATHEMATICAL LITERACY	• What is mathematics? • How can mathematics be used to understand and analyze data, numbers, patterns, functions, measurements, reasoning, and relationships quantitatively, spatially, and statistically? • How can mathematics be used as an instrument, a language, a way to transfer mathematical knowledge and thinking, and to encourage its use?
SCIENTIFIC LITERACY	• What is science? • How does science explain our world? • How can science be used to discover answers to questions derived from curiosity about everyday experiences? • How does science describe, explain, and predict natural phenomena?
HISTORICAL LITERACY	• How is history both a description and interpretation of the past? • How does history provide a sense of chronology and understanding of incidents, individuals, and issues in our physical world? • How do the historical experiences of societies, people, and nations reveal patterns of continuity and change? • How does understanding history involve research and drawing conclusions backed up with evidentiary support?
SOCIAL LITERACY	• How does the study of culture assist in the examination of social beliefs, values, institutions, behaviors, traditions, and ways of life? • What influences do people, places, groups, institutions, and environments have on each other? • What is the relationship between science, technology, and society? • What does it mean to be a contributing member of society globally, nationally, and locally?
ARTISTIC LITERACY	• How are artistic ideas conceived and developed? • How can artistic ideas and works be interpreted, presented, realized, and shared? • How do the arts convey meaning? • How can artistic ideas and work be related to personal meaning and external context?
HEALTH LITERACY	• How can good health be enhanced and promoted? • How can health risks be avoided or reduced? • How can life skills, including interpersonal communication, decision making, and goal setting, be used to enhance good health?

Figure 2.4   Good Essential Questions: Rational Numbers

ESSENTIAL	Universal	• How is life defined by connections, patterns, relationships, and systems?
	Overarching	• How can mathematics be used to understand and evaluate data, numbers, patterns, functions, measurements, patterns, reasoning, and relationships fluently, quantitatively, spatially, symmetrically, measurably, and statistically? • How can mathematical representations be created and used to organize, record, and use mathematical ideas? • How can numbers be represented? • What is the relationship between numbers and number systems?
	Topical	• How can numbers not be rational, and how can they be approximated using rational numbers?

	Driving	• How can *you* use rational approximations of irrational numbers to do the following?
		  - Compare the size of irrational numbers.
		  - Locate them approximately on a number line diagram.
		  - Estimate the value of expressions (e.g., π^2).
		• How can *you* use square root and cube root symbols to represent solutions to equations of the form $x^2 = p$ and $x^3 = p$ where p is a positive rational number?

Notice how the essential questions for this unit scaffold from reflecting upon abstract ideas about mathematics, to examining a broader conceptual understanding of the number system, to addressing more specific concepts of rational and irrational numbers. The topical question establishes the instructional goal and evaluates the depth and extent of students' understanding. In the process, students solve mathematical problems that serve as examples and strengthen their responses to the topical question.

Topical questions in English language arts focus on specific texts that are often reviewed in class. These topical questions also consider how universal ideas and themes are addressed and what conventions of literacy and language are used to present information. For example, a good topical question about a specific work of fiction or nonfiction will challenge students to demonstrate their deeper understanding of key ideas, the particular craft and structure, and how the text presents certain ideas. Consider the following scenario.

You are teaching a book study on *Charlotte's Web* by E. B. White. Your students are expected to do the following:

- Determine central ideas or themes of a text and analyze their development; summarize the key supporting details and ideas. (CCSS.ELA-LITERACY.CCRA.R.2)

- Analyze how and why individuals, events, or ideas develop and interact over the course of a text. (CCSS.ELA-LITERACY.CCRA.R.3)

- Assess how point of view or purpose shapes the content and style of a text. (CCSS.ELA-LITERACY.CCRA.R.6)

- Integrate and evaluate content presented in diverse media and formats, including visually and quantitatively, as well as in words. (CCSS.ELA-LITERACY.CCRA.R.7)

- Write narratives to develop real or imagined experiences or events using effective technique, well-chosen details, and well-structured event sequences. (CCSS.ELA-LITERACY.CCRA.W.3)

- Draw evidence from literary or informational texts to support analysis, reflection, and research. (CCSS.ELA-LITERACY.CCRA.W.9)

Your students will address and respond to the good questions in Figure 2.5.

Figure 2.5   Good Essential Questions: *Charlotte's Web*

ESSENTIAL	Universal	• What is friendship?
	Overarching	• How can the central ideas or themes of a text be determined? • How do the central ideas and themes of a text develop? • How do individuals, events, and ideas develop and interact over the course of a text? • How do authors express and share their point of view through text? • How does point of view or purpose shape the content and style of a text? • How can content be integrated in diverse media and formats visually, quantitatively, and verbally? • How do narratives share real or imagined experiences or events using effective technique, well-chosen details, and well-structured event sequences?
	Topical	• How does *Charlotte's Web* by E. B. White address the theme of friendship—specifically, the unlikely friendship between characters who are very different from each other?
	Driving	• What kind of original narrative can *you* produce that tells about the unlikely friendship between two characters who are very different from each other?

These good questions guide students to a deeper learning experience and expand their technical understanding of how reading and writing promotes learning. Students also expand their thinking about broader ideas and themes—in this case, *what is friendship*. The overarching question also sets the instructional objective of the lesson or unit. For this lesson, the instructional objective is to explain how *Charlotte's Web* addresses the theme of friendship—specifically, the unlikely friendship between the two main characters.

Of the four types of essential questions, topical questions are the ones that directly address grade-level standards and subjects. They also provide students the opportunity to demonstrate the depth of their knowledge and thinking about what they have learned. Student responses need to be in-depth explanations with specific supports.

Driving Essential Questions

Driving questions require students to share their insights and learning in their own unique way. These good questions challenge students to think creatively and strategically about what they can create, design, develop, do, plan, or produce, based on the depth of their knowledge. Driving questions also encourage students to explore content through the following active learning experiences:

- Project-based learning that prompts students to demonstrate the depth of their learning through oral, written, creative, or technical expression.
- Inquiry-based learning that engages students to delve deeper into the concepts and content through research, examination, and design.
- Problem-based learning that challenges students to transfer and use what they have learned to address, settle, or solve a variety of academic and real-world problems.
- Expeditionary learning that encourages students to examine how the academic concepts they are learning are applicable in the real world.
- Service learning that prompts students to use what they have learned to contribute or give back to their community globally, nationally, and locally.

These instructional methods and strategies challenge students to present and share their expertise—the self-knowledge and personal skills they develop through their education and experiences. They also reflect how students will be expected to transfer and use their expertise in the real world—by designing projects, conducting investigations, addressing problems and issues, and contributing to their community. Let's take a look at how good essential questions turn students into experts and specialists in a particular area or topic.

English Language Arts, Fine Arts, Visual Arts

In English language arts and in the fine and performing arts, good driving questions transition students from thinking like a critic who analyzes and evaluates texts to thinking like a creator who produces original work. Consider how the following scenario encourages students to express their own creativity.

You are teaching a genre study on historical fiction. Your students are expected to do the following:

- Read closely to determine what the text says explicitly and to make logical inferences from it; cite specific textual evidence when writing or speaking to support conclusions drawn from the text. (CCSS.ELA-LITERACY.CCRA.R.1)

- Determine central ideas or themes of a text and analyze their development; summarize the key supporting details and ideas. (CCSS.ELA-LITERACY.CCRA.R.2)

- Assess how point of view or purpose shapes the content and style of a text. (CCSS.ELA-LITERACY.CCRA.R.6)

- Analyze how two or more texts address similar themes or topics in order to build knowledge or compare the approaches the authors take. (CCSS.ELA-LITERACY.CCRA.R.9)

- Write narratives to develop real or imagined experiences or events using effective technique, well-chosen details, and well-structured event sequences. (CCSS.ELA-LITERACY.CCRA.W.3)

- Conduct short research projects to answer a question drawing on several sources; generate additional related questions for further research and investigation. (CCSS.ELA-LITERACY.CCRA.W.7)

- Present information, findings, and supporting evidence such that listeners can follow the line of reasoning and the organization, development, and style are appropriate to task, purpose, and audience. (CCSS.ELA-LITERACY.CCRA.SL.4)

Your students will address the good questions in Figure 2.6.

Note the transition between the topical question and the driving question in Figure 2.6 (p. 34). The topical question prompts students to critique the historical fiction works they are reading. The driving question provides students the opportunity to create their own original work of historical fiction using the technical knowledge they have developed during reading and writing narratives. By addressing the driving question, students develop a deeper appreciation of the universal ideas explored—in particular, how and why authors write and share their ideas.

Mathematics

Good driving questions teach students to think like mathematicians by challenging them to consider how they can use mathematics in different academic and

Figure 2.6   Good Essential Questions: Historical Fiction

ESSENTIAL	Universal	• How and why do authors write and share their perspectives or point of view? • How many sides are there to a story? • What constitutes the truth? • How do we learn about life in the past? • What can the past teach us and how can we learn from it? • Whose "story" is history? • Is history a factual depiction or a particular interpretation?
	Overarching	• How can the central ideas or themes of a text be determined? • How do the central ideas and themes of a text develop over the course of a text? • How does point of view or purpose shape the content and style of a text? • How can two or more texts address similar themes or topics to build knowledge?
	Topical	• How can a fictional portrayal of a historical time, place, event, or individual and a historical account of the same period serve as a means to understand history?
	Driving	• What kind of original narrative text of historical fiction can you produce that balances fact and fiction about an actual historical time, place, event, or individual?

real-world situations. This change in thinking transitions students from learning and doing math as an abstract exercise to understanding math's potential to solve practical, observable problems. Consider how the following scenario engages students to communicate what they can design and produce with geometric figures.

You are teaching a unit on drawing, constructing, and describing the relationship between geometric figures. Your students are expected to do the following:

- Solve problems involving scale drawings of geometric figures, including computing actual lengths and areas from a scale drawing and reproducing a scale drawing at a different scale. (CCSS.MATH.CONTENT.7.G.A.1)

- Draw (freehand, with ruler and protractor, and with technology) geometric shapes with given conditions. Focus on constructing triangles from three measures of angles or sides, noticing when the conditions determine a unique triangle, more than one triangle, or no triangle. (CCSS.MATH.CONTENT.7.G.A.2)

- Describe the two-dimensional figures that result from slicing three-dimensional figures, as in plane sections of right rectangular prisms and right rectangular pyramids. (CCSS.MATH.CONTENT.7.G.A.3)

Your students will respond to the good essential questions in Figure 2.7.

Figure 2.7   Good Essential Questions: Geometry

	Universal	• How can the forms and patterns of objects in life be described and determined?
ESSENTIAL	Overarching	• How can mathematical ideas be categorized, classified, comprehended, and communicated? • How and why can the characteristics and properties of two- and three-dimensional geometric shapes be analyzed? • How can visualization, spatial reasoning, and geometric modeling be used to solve problems?
	Topical	• How can geometrical figures and the relationships among them be constructed and described?
	Driving	• How can you construct geometrical figures and describe the relationship among them? • What kind of original or scale design, drawing, construct, or model could *you* produce using geometric figures and how would *you* explain the relationship among the figures in your design?

Notice how driving questions prompt students to create, do, or produce something based on what they have learned about geometrical figures. The driving questions also encourage students to share what kind of original design, drawing, or model they personally could produce using geometric figures and to explain the relationship between the figures they chose. The exercise prompts students to demonstrate creative thinking in mathematics and communicate their knowledge at the most comprehensive levels of cognitive rigor.

Science

Driving questions in science support STEM education by engaging students to think like scientists and engineers. Derive these good questions from performance objectives and engage students in using the scientific method or the engineering design process to explain natural phenomenon. For example, what kind of explanation can you construct, what kind of data or evidence can you provide, or what kind of model could you develop and use? Consider the following scenario.

You are teaching a unit on changes, processes, and reactions in matter and substances. Your students are expected to do the following:

• Develop models to describe the atomic composition of simple molecules and extended structures. (NGSS-MS-PS1-1)

- Analyze and interpret data on the properties of substances before and after the substances interact to determine if a chemical reaction has occurred. (NGSS-MS-PS1-2)

- Gather and make sense of information on the natural resources origins of synthetic materials and their impact on society. (NGSS-MS-PS1-3)

- Develop a model that predicts and describes changes in particle motion, temperature, and state of a pure substance when thermal energy is added or removed. (NGSS-MS-PS1-4)

- Develop and use a model to describe how the total number of atoms does not change in a chemical reaction and thus mass is conserved. (NGSS-MS-PS1-5)

- Undertake a design project to construct, test, and modify a device that either releases or absorbs thermal energy by chemical processes. (NGSS-MS-PS1-6)

Your students will address the good questions in Figure 2.8.

Figure 2.8   Good Essential Questions: Atomic and Molecular Structures

ESSENTIAL	**Universal**	• How can life be organized and characterized? • What is the relationship between forms and events in patterns? • How is life an endless cycle of causes and effects?
	Overarching	• How are macroscopic patterns related to the nature of microscopic and atomic-level structures? • How can cause-and-effect relationships be used to predict phenomena in natural or designed systems? • How can models be used to observe time, space, and energy phenomena at various scales and systems that are too large or too small? • How and why can matter be conserved in physical and chemical processes due to the conservation of atoms? • How does the transfer of energy drive the motion and cycling of matter?
	Topical	• How can the structure, properties, and interactions of matter be explained?
	Driving	• How can *you* develop and use a model to describe the atomic composition of simple molecules and extended structures? • How can you develop and use a model that describes and predicts changes in the particle motion, temperature, and state of a pure substance when thermal energy is added or removed? • What kind of model could *you* develop and use to describe how the total number of atoms does not change in a chemical reaction and thus mass is conserved? • What kind of design project could *you* undertake to test and modify a device that either releases or absorbs thermal energy by chemical processes?

Notice how the driving questions directly address the performance objectives of these college- and career-ready standards and engage students to communicate how their research, investigation, and design are similar to those of scientists and engineers. The questions also expand student knowledge about science and engineering and how experts in those fields examine and explain natural events and phenomena.

History and Social Studies

Good questions teach students to think like historians by engaging them in expressing their thoughts about how ideas, incidents, individuals, and issues affect the world. Consider how the following scenario engages students to establish their own arguments and conclusions about the impact of actions and decisions made following the American Revolution.

You are teaching a unit on government formation at the national and state levels following the American Revolution. Your students are expected to do the following:

- Assess the importance of the Northwest Ordinance. (NHS.USE3.2.A.4)

- Use, organize, and integrate applicable evidence from multiple relevant sources and interpretations into a coherent, reasoned argument about the past. (C3.D2.His.16)

Your students will respond to the good questions in Figure 2.9.

Consider the cognitive rigor of the driving question on the Northwest Ordinance (p. 38). Instead of simply reporting the facts or repeating the conclusions of others, this good question encourages students to present their own argument about this document's long-lasting effects using the information provided by credible sources. Good driving questions engage students in actively learning about history by critiquing ideas and events rather than by restating other people's ideas and conclusions. These questions encourage students to think creatively and share what they can create, do, or produce based on their own knowledge in a particular field of study.

How Can We Teach Using Good Essential Questions?

Good universal questions serve as the entry points to various learning experiences. They can be used to engage students in class dialogues, small group discussions, or journal prompts. When asking universal questions, stress that free expression is more important than being correct, but students should be prepared to defend their responses with evidence derived from either their education or experience.

Figure 2.9   Good Essential Questions: The Northwest Ordinance

ESSENTIAL	**Universal**	• What are our basic yet essential liberties and rights? • How do governments "fail" or regimes "fall"? • Why do we study the past? • What influence does the past have on the present?
	Overarching	• How can historical events be classified as examples of past and current change? • How can applicable evidence from multiple interpretations be used, organized, and integrated into a coherent, reasoned argument about the past?
	Topical	• How did the Northwest Ordinance address how the Northwest Territory of the United States was to be governed? • How did the Northwest Ordinance establish the guidelines for when and how parts of the territory attained statehood?

	Driving	• What kind of historical argument can you make for the impact of the Northwest Ordinance on the following?
		  - The development and addition of new states
		  - The definition of U.S. citizenship
		  - The balance of power among the states and the federal government
		  - A clear definition of basic yet essential liberties
		  - Restrictions on slavery
		  - Provisions for public education
		  - The "Utmost Good Faith" clause for Native Americans

Good overarching questions are appropriate for any grade level. The number of good overarching questions will vary depending upon how extensively a specific lesson addresses the core ideas in a subject area. Use these questions to evaluate students' background or knowledge in a subject area. Good overarching questions may serve as benchmark or summative assessments that mark and measure progressive or cumulative learning in a particular class, grade, or subject.

Topical questions serve as the bookends for a single lesson or entire unit, setting the instructional focus and serving as the summative assessment for student learning. Pose these questions at the beginning of the learning experience to inform students of how extensively they will be required to address a particular text or topic. Then present topical questions at the end of the lesson or unit as the summative assessment. Limit the topical essential questions to one or two good questions that truly mark and measure the depth and extent that students are expected to learn about the subject matter. We want our students to develop and demonstrate deeper knowledge and thinking, but don't want to overwhelm them.

Good driving questions allow students to create, develop, do, present, or produce something with their acquired knowledge. The outcome can be an argument, a critique, a design, an invention, a model, a plan, a project, a problem, a service, a solution, or a text that reflects the depth of their learning. Good driving questions should always allow students to demonstrate the depth and detail of their learning in their own unique way, which is the ultimate goal of teaching for cognitive rigor.

Conclusion

The intent and purpose of good essential questions are to establish the instructional focus and expectations of the lesson or unit. They also engage students to think deeply and share the depth and extent of their learning. Individually, each essential question challenges students to develop and demonstrate broader awareness (universal), conceptual understanding (overarching), subject knowledge (topical), and personal expertise (driving). When used collectively, these good questions will establish a deep, student-centered learning experience that is both active and authentic.

PROFESSIONAL DEVELOPMENT

How to Develop Good Essential Questions That Set the Instructional Focus and Serve as the Summative Assessment for Lessons and Units

Objective

Develop good essential questions that set the instructional focus and serve as formative and summative assessments for learning.

Materials

- College- and career-ready standards adopted by your state
- Curriculum and texts adopted by your school
- Good Questions and Bloom's Taxonomy (Figure 1.2)
- Good Questions and Depth of Knowledge (Figure 1.4)

Procedure

1. Determine the broader ideas addressed in the texts and the topics being reviewed in class. Place these ideas framed as questions in the Universal category in Figure 2.10.

2. Identify the anchor standards (ELA/fine arts), standards and practices (math), cross-cutting concepts (science), or disciplinary concepts (history/social studies) that will be addressed. Rephrase the performance objectives into good questions and place them in the Overarching category. (Use Figure 1.7, p. 23, to rephrase the performance objectives.)

3. Choose the cluster or the standard that sets the instructional expectation for the lesson or unit. Rephrase the performance objective into a good question that asks *how, why,* or *what causes,* and place it in the Topical category. This question will serve as the instructional focus and summative assessment for the lesson or unit. (Use Figure 1.7, p. 23, to rephrase the performance objectives.)

4. Choose a standard that tasks students to *do something* (e.g., apply, conduct, construct, create, design, develop, do, find, invent, innovate, modify, prepare, present, produce, use, or write). Rephrase the performance objective into a good question that asks *what can* you *create, design, develop, do, plan,* or *produce;* or *how could* or *how would* you *create, design, develop, do, plan,* or *produce;* and place the rephrased question into the Driving category. This question will serve as the driving question that prompts students to create, design, do, or produce something that reflects and represents the depth and extent of their learning. (Use Figure 1.7, p. 23 to rephrase the performance objectives.)

Figure 2.10   Good Essential Questions Generator

ESSENTIAL	**UNIVERSAL** What ideas, issues, themes, or topics are raised?	
	OVERARCHING What are the core ideas of the academic subject that will be expanded upon?	
	TOPICAL What are the key understandings that will be examined, explored, and explained?	
	DRIVING How will deeper learning be demonstrated and communicated in depth, insightfully, and inimitably using oral, written, creative, or technical expression?	

3

How Do Good Factual Questions Set the Foundation for Deeper Learning?

You are teaching an author study on Edgar Allan Poe. Your students are expected to do the following:

- Determine central ideas or themes of a text and analyze their development; summarize the key supporting details and ideas. (CCSS.ELA-LITERACY.CCRA.R.2)

- Analyze the structure of texts, including how specific sentences, paragraphs, and larger portions of the text (e.g., a section, chapter, scene, or stanza) relate to each other and the whole. (CCSS.ELA-LITERACY.CCRA.R.5)

- Analyze how two or more texts address similar themes or topics in order to build knowledge or to compare the approaches the authors take. (CCSS.ELA-LITERACY. CCRA.R.9)

- Write narratives to develop real or imagined experiences or events using effective technique, well-chosen details, and well-structured event sequences. (CCSS. ELA-LITERACY.CCRA.W.3)

- Draw evidence from literary or informational texts to support analysis, reflection, and research. (CCSS.ELA-LITERACY.CCRA.W.9)

To start the author study, ask your students the good questions in Figure 3.1.

We typically ask students the questions outlined in Figure 3.1 after they read one of Poe's stories or at the end of a lesson or unit to assess their understanding of the topic. But what if we pose these questions at the beginning of the lesson or before students read one of Poe's stories? What if we also direct students to research the factual information they need to know instead of directly telling them?

Figure 3.1   Good Factual Questions: Edgar Allan Poe

FACTUAL	What is gothic literature? Who was Edgar Allan Poe? What did Edgar Allan Poe write? When did Edgar Allan Poe write and publish his literary fiction and nonfiction? What are considered to be Poe's exemplary and groundbreaking works? What is the plot of Edgar Allan Poe's stories and poems? What is the general setting of Edgar Allan Poe's stories and poems? Who are the character archetypes in Edgar Allan Poe's stories? What are the gothic archetypes featured in Edgar Allan Poe's stories? What are the common ideas, motifs, symbols, and themes in Poe's works? What are Edgar Allan Poe's three theories about literature according to his essay "The Philosophy of Composition"?

Factual questions address just what the name says—the facts about texts and topics. Answering such questions traditionally acts as what Cunningham (1987) calls "exercises in rote memory" that assess whether students can recall explicitly what they have learned (p. 71). With teaching and learning for cognitive rigor, good factual questions indicate what information is essential and relevant to build students' background knowledge and support their thinking abilities.

What Good Factual Questions Do

Good factual questions focus primarily on the details of the content in a particular academic area or discipline (Krathwohl, 2002). The cognitive rigor of these questions addresses the lower end of the Bloom and Webb frameworks by expecting students to correctly recall and reproduce specific information presented by a teacher or in a provided text (Anderson & Krathwohl, 2001; Webb, 2002; Hess et al., 2009a).

Traditionally, good factual questions generally ask students to remember, recall, and recognize who, what, where, or when. In classrooms that promote cognitive rigor, good factual questions serve as the launching pad for deeper learning. These questions are both instructional and evaluative inquiries that ask students to do the following:

• **Define** and **describe** the meaning of words and terminology in detail and in depth.

• **Read**, **review, and rephrase** the details and ideas presented in text accurately and authentically.

Recognize, research, and **retrieve** information from textual sources to use as evidence to strengthen and support their learning.

With cognitive rigor, good factual questions challenge students to recognize and understand essential and relevant information presented in texts and topics, which is actually a higher cognitive demand than remembering and recalling. These question stems are typically categorized as a DOK-1 because they expect students to recall and reproduce data, definitions, and details. They are also generally considered to be the most difficult for students to answer because it takes a lot of time and effort to remember the vast amount of information as accurately and explicitly as it was taught. However, with cognitive rigor, the question's level of difficulty depends more on how much time and effort is needed to read, research, and record the information they have acquired by paraphrasing, transcribing, or citing sources.

Don't misunderstand my statement—students must still remember and recall what they are learning, and factual questions are an effective means for assessing and evaluating these cognitive actions. Remembering and recalling, however, are more about knowledge assessment, not knowledge acquisition. Knowledge acquisition involves reading, researching, and recognizing what needs to be known and understood—and recording that information by paraphrasing, transcribing, and citing examples. The instructional goal of good factual questions is to guide students in acquiring and gathering information so they can process it into deeper knowledge and understanding. Eventually we want them to transfer the information and use it in depth, insightfully, and in their own unique ways. We can assess how well they remember and recall what they have learned by seeing how they use the knowledge they have developed to address and respond to more complex questions.

Vocabulary Knowledge and Development

One of the most important aspects of teaching for cognitive rigor is the sharing of knowledge. This requires students to develop a deeper understanding of the meaning and use of words and terms. Factual questions expect students to communicate what the words mean and "how [these words] interconnect [and create] networks of knowledge that allow students to connect new information to previously learned information" (Marzano & Simms, 2013, p. 5). They also provide students with a foundational knowledge they can draw upon when asked to demonstrate deeper thinking such as when categorizing, inferencing, and summarizing (Anderson & Pearson, 1984; Kintsch, 1998; Kintsch & van Dijk, 1978; Marzano & Simms, 2013; Stahl & Stahl, 2012). Consider how good factual questions in the following example help students develop a fundamental knowledge of multiplication by explaining different terms correlated to mathematical concepts.

You are teaching a unit on representing and solving problems using multiplication. Your students are expected to do the following:

- Interpret products of whole numbers. (CCSS.MATH.CONTENT.3.OA.A.1)

- Use multiplication and division within 100 to solve word problems in situations involving equal groups, arrays, and measurement quantities, e.g., by using drawings and equations with a symbol for the unknown number to represent the problem. (CCSS.MATH.CONTENT.3.OA.A.3)

- Determine the unknown whole number in a multiplication or division equation relating three whole numbers. (CCSS.MATH.CONTENT.3.OA.A.4)

The students will respond to the good questions as detailed in Figure 3.2.

Figure 3.2   Good Factual Questions: Multiplication

FACTUAL	What does it mean to interpret?
	What does it mean to determine?
	What does it mean to represent?
	What does it mean to multiply?
	What is a whole number?
	What is multiplication?
	What is the multiplier in a multiplication problem and where is it located?
	What is the multiplicand in a multiplication problem and where is it located?
	What is the product of a multiplication problem?
	What is a factor in a multiplication problem?
	What is the unknown number in a multiplication problem?
	What is an equal group?
	What is an array?
	What are measurement quantities?
	What are the properties of operations in multiplication?

Notice how these factual questions require students to define the different domain or subject-specific terminology related to multiplication—specifically, what it is, what it does, and where it is located. The questions also require students to define both the mathematical terminology and the common academic vocabulary that will likely be encountered in other curricula (e.g., to interpret, to determine, and to apply). Students should be challenged to define and describe these terms in their own words rather than verbatim from the text or teacher. We'll get to how students should address and respond to factual questions later in this chapter.

Close Reading of Texts

Factual questions are typically used to assess whether students understand the basic details and ideas presented in the texts they read—specifically, what happens, where it happens, when it happens, and who is involved. These questions promote cognitive rigor by guiding students to recognize and refer to the relevant information in the text that will support their analyses and arguments. Consider how the following good factual questions prompt students to cite specific information from two famous civil rights leaders.

You are teaching a lesson that requires students to compare and contrast the philosophies of Martin Luther King Jr. and Malcolm X. Your students are expected to do the following:

- Classify and analyze a series of historical events or developments as examples of change over time. (C3.D2.His.2.6-12)

- Use questions generated about individuals and groups to analyze why the developments they helped shape are seen as historically significant and assess how the significance of their actions changed over time and is shaped by historical context. (C3.D2.His.3.6-12)

- Explain why individuals and groups differ in their perspective of the same historical period due to various and often complex, interacting factors. (C3.D2.His.4.6-12)

- Analyze how and why perspectives of people have changed over time and how historical contexts still continue to shape people's perspectives. (C3.D2.His.5.6-12)

- Analyze the leadership and ideology of Martin Luther King Jr. and Malcolm X in the Civil Rights Movement and evaluate their legacies. (NHS.USE9.4.A.4)

- Determine central ideas or themes of a text and analyze the development; summarize the key supporting details and ideas. (CCSS.ELA-LITERACY.CCRA.R.2)

- Assess how point of view or purpose shapes the content and style of a text. (CCSS.ELA-LITERACY.CCRA.R.6)

- Delineate and evaluate the argument and specific claims in a text, including the validity of the reasoning as well as the relevance and sufficiency of the evidence. (CCSS.ELA-LITERACY.CCRA.R.8)

Your students are expected to address the good questions in Figure 3.3.

Figure 3.3   Good Factual Questions: Martin Luther King Jr.

FACTUAL	Who was Martin Luther King Jr. and what was his role in the civil rights movement? Who was Malcolm X and what was his role in the civil rights movement? When did Martin Luther King Jr. and Malcolm X advocate and march for civil rights? What do Martin Luther King Jr. and Malcolm X say explicitly about the following? • Fighting for equality • The role of whites in the Civil Rights Movement • Integration • Violence

Factual questions are highly text-dependent in that they can only be addressed with specific details from a specific source—in this case, what Martin Luther King Jr. and Malcolm X say about fighting for equality, integration, and the role of whites in the civil rights movement. This information deepens students' understanding about the central ideas of these texts and serves to support their responses. Students should respond to these questions by either paraphrasing or by directly quoting and properly citing specific statements made in speeches by these leaders.

Informational Literacy

Students must develop the skills of how to access, evaluate, and use the information they gather (Friedman, 2005; Trilling & Fadel, 2009; Wagner, 2014). These are the cognitive actions associated with research—one of the essential skills that students will use frequently in their lives. Good factual questions tell students what to look for and how to acquire the information they need from credible sources, whether print or electronic. Consider how these good factual questions encourage students to research information about Earth and the solar system beyond what their teacher or textbook presents.

You are teaching students about the role gravity plays in the relationship among Earth, the moon, the sun, and other celestial bodies in the solar system. Your students are expected to do the following:

- Develop and use a model of the Earth-sun-moon system to describe the cyclic patterns of lunar phases, eclipses of the sun and moon, and seasons. (NGSS-MS-ESS1-1)

- Develop and use a model to describe the role of gravity in the motions within galaxies and the solar system. (NGSS-MS-ESS1-2)

- Analyze and interpret data to determine scale properties of objects in the solar system. (NGSS-MS-ESS1-3)

Your students will address and respond to the questions noted in Figure 3.4.

Figure 3.4   Good Factual Questions: Astronomy

FACTUAL	What is a celestial object and where are such objects located?
	What is a galaxy and where can one be found?
	What are the celestial objects in our solar system?
	What is Earth?
	What is the moon?
	What is the sun?
	What are lunar phases and when do they occur?
	What are seasons and when do they occur?
	What is a solar eclipse and when can it occur?
	What is a lunar eclipse and when can it occur?
	What is gravity?

The instructional focus of these good questions is for students to define and describe the details and terminology addressed in the performance objectives. Students enter these questions into online search engines to acquire the background knowledge and textual evidence they need to support their response to more complex questions. They should not only paraphrase and transcribe the information they gather, but also determine *what is the reliability of the information source* and *what determines whether a source is reliable* (which is another set of good questions that can be addressed as part of this unit or as a separate lesson).

Good factual questions make knowledge acquisition more active and engaging because they prompt students to seek what they need to learn by researching and rephrasing the information they must acquire. When students respond to good questions, they learn how to be proactive and self-sufficient instead of passively receiving what they need to know from teachers. Students need to develop self-sufficiency because it will help them succeed academically, personally, professionally, and socially.

Teaching Using Good Factual Questions

Asking good factual questions focuses students' attention on acquiring and gathering the most essential and most relevant information from a lesson. Typically, teachers point out exactly what needs to be known and where this information can be found, and students repeat the information verbatim. Good questions rooted in cognitive rigor principles require students to spend the time and energy to delve deeper into who, what, where, or when. They also challenge students to share this information accurately and authentically by paraphrasing information or transcribing specific descriptions and details with the credible sources properly cited.

Consider how the following good questions prompt students to the research information needed to fully understand World War II.

You are teaching a unit on the causes and global consequences of World War II. Your students are expected to do the following:

- Understand the causes and global consequences of World War II. (NHS.WHE8.2)

- Understand major global trends from 1900 to the end of World War II. (NHS. WHE8.5.A)

- Create and use a chronological sequence to analyze how historical events were shaped by unique circumstances of time and place as well as the broader historical contexts in which they occurred. (C3.D2.His.1)

- Compare the perspectives of people in the past to those of people today and explain how each group's unique set of historical factors influenced their perspectives. (C3. D2.His.4)

- Explain and analyze multiple and complex causes and effects of events in the past. (C3.D2.His.14)

- Evaluate and develop a historical argument focused on the relative influence of various causes of a past event and distinguish between long-term causes and the contemporary triggering events. (C3.D2.His.15)

Your students will respond to the good questions in Figure 3.5.

The questions in Figure 3.5 expect students to learn a vast amount of factual information. In a classroom focused on promoting cognitive rigor, however, we wouldn't ask students to recall all this information. Rather, the purpose of questioning would be to encourage students to read and research the background knowledge they need to address more complex questions and to develop their historical arguments for the lesson. The responses to these questions should be paraphrased statements or properly cited transcriptions from credible sources, not just copied straight from the printed or electronic page. Recording and rephrasing this information will not only help students remember the specific details and facts correctly but also engage them in thinking critically about how they can share this information clearly, comprehensively, and creatively for later review.

Figure 3.5   Good Factual Questions: World War II

FACTUAL	What is a total war? What is fascism? What is imperialism? What is an authoritarian or totalitarian regime? What is nationalism? What is national socialism? What is communism? What is materialism? What is isolationism? What is Nazism? When did World War II occur and what was the timeframe? What were the ideologies, policies, and governing methods of totalitarian regimes prior to and during World War II? Who were the Axis Powers and which nations belonged to this group? Who were the Allied Powers and which nations belonged to this group? What were the wartime aims and strategies of the Allied Powers? Who were the key individuals and leaders involved in World War II?

Teachers also use good factual questions to teach vocabulary through "frequent exposures to the words, encounters in multiple contexts, and deep or active processing of the words" (McKeown, Beck, & Apthorp, 2010, p. 1; quoted in Marzano & Simms, 2013, p. 10).

Consider how the following good factual questions prompt students to define the subject-specific terminology correlated to geometric measurements using volume.

You are teaching a unit on understanding volume. Your students are expected to do the following:

- Recognize volume as an attribute of solid figures and understand concepts of volume measurement. (CCSS.MATH.CONTENT.5.MD.C.3)

- Measure volumes by counting unit cubes, using cubic cm., cubic in., cubic ft., and improvised units. (CCSS.MATH.CONTENT.5.MD.C.4)

- Relate volume to the operations of multiplication and addition and solve real world and mathematical problems involving volume. (CCSS.MATH.CONTENT.5.MD.C.5)

Your students will address the good questions in Figure 3.6.

Figure 3.6   Good Factual Questions: Volume

FACTUAL	What is volume? What is a unit cube? What is the side length of a cube? What is a cubic unit? What is a right rectangular prism? What is the edge length of a right rectangular prism? What are threefold whole-number products? What is additive? What does the formula $V = l \times w \times h$ measure, and when is it used? What does the formula $V = b \times h$ measure, and when is it used?

Notice how the first performance objective listed in Figure 3.6 calls for students to answer two "what" questions—what is volume and what are the concepts of volume measurement. To meet the cognitive demands of the subsequent standards, students must be able to answer several more factual questions—what are unit cubes and cubic units. Students need this information to measure volume. They should also be challenged to paraphrase the definition in their own words to demonstrate and communicate their deep knowledge and genuine understanding of the terms. Students can use the examples and problems provided by the text or teacher to strengthen and support their responses.

To solve real-world problems, students also must learn the definitions of academic vocabulary words (i.e., additive) and subject-specific terminology such as right rectangular prism, threefold whole-number products, and edge lengths. They must also understand the specific formulas for measuring volume ($V = l \times w \times h$ and $V = b \times h$) and when to use these formulas. Explicitly teach these words and terms so that students have a clear understanding of the knowledge required to solve algorithmic and word problems. Encourage students to record and report this information in their own words and to use examples and problems from the text as supporting evidence.

With content-driven subjects such as history, science, and social studies, students are expected to define and describe the terms and topics identified within the academic standards or curriculum requirements. Consider how the topics of factual questions are drawn from the following content-driven academic standards.

You are teaching a unit on ecosystem, interactions, energy, and dynamics. Your students will do the following:

- Analyze and interpret data to provide evidence for the effects of resource availability on organisms and populations of organisms in an ecosystem. (NGSS-MS-LS2-1)

- Construct an explanation that predicts patterns of interactions among organisms across multiple ecosystems. (NGSS-MS-LS2-2)

- Develop a model to describe the cycling of matter and flow of energy among living and nonliving parts of an ecosystem. (NGSS-MS-LS2-3)

- Construct an argument supported by empirical evidence that changes to physical or biological components of an ecosystem affect populations. (NGSS-MS-LS2-4)

- Evaluate competing design solutions for maintaining biodiversity and ecosystem services. (NGSS-MS-LS2-5)

The students will address the good questions in Figure 3.7.

Figure 3.7   Good Factual Questions: Ecosystems

FACTUAL	What is an organism?
	What is an ecosystem?
	What is the structure of an ecosystem?
	What are the resources available to organisms and to populations of organisms in an ecosystem?
	What are the physical and biological components of an ecosystem?
	What does *biotic* mean and what are examples of biotic characteristics of an ecosystem?
	What does *abiotic* mean and what are examples of abiotic characteristics of an ecosystem?
	What are the different forms of matter and energy that exist within and sustain an ecosystem?

Notice how the good factual questions for this unit on ecosystems ask students to research the subject matter addressed in the academic standards and the cognitive demands of the performance objectives. Also, note how the factual questions for the unit are similar to the ones on World War II and the unit on the role of gravity. Challenge students to use the credible sources provided in the curriculum or encourage them to look for other credible sources for the essential information they need to develop and demonstrate deep knowledge and understanding.

Of the questions that teachers ask as part of a learning experience, factual questions are the easiest to develop, present, and grade. They are also the simplest questions to ask because they focus primarily on the concrete details, elements, and terminology in the texts that students are reading. We can use factual questions to identify the essential and relevant information that students need to recognize and understand; however, we can use those same questions to teach students how to acquire and gather information through reading and research—two essential skills they must develop to be college- and career-ready.

Conclusion

Asking factual questions has been the standard way to assess student learning. Asking *good* factual questions expands students' knowledge and extends their thinking beyond recalling "the stuff" they learned. Teachers can use factual questions at the beginning of a lesson to gauge students' background knowledge. Asked during a learning experience, these questions function as checks for understanding. Asked at the end of an educational experience, good questions allow teachers to evaluate how well students remember key content. As a result, good factual questions inform students about the depth of the knowledge they need to acquire to succeed.

PROFESSIONAL DEVELOPMENT
How to Develop Good Factual Questions

Objective

Develop good factual questions that inform students about gathering, researching and retrieving *the essential information* they need to think deeper about concepts and content.

Materials

- College- and career-ready standards adopted by your state
- Curriculum and texts adopted by your school
- Good Questions and Bloom's Taxonomy (Figure 1.2)
- Good Questions and Depth of Knowledge (Figure 1.4)

Procedure

1. Identify the academic standards, texts, and topics that will be addressed as part of the lesson or unit.

2. Identify *what is the academic vocabulary and subject-specific terminology* addressed in the standards or the curriculum students must define or describe. List those terms in the row marked Vocabulary Knowledge in Figure 3.8.

3. Identify *what are the specific details and elements* in the text that students must recognize and understand. List those details in the row marked Close Reading with the appropriate HOT Stem (e.g., *who, what, where, when*).

4. Identify *what is the essential and relevant information* students must recognize, research, and retrieve to support their knowledge and thinking. List that information in the row marked Information Literacy with the appropriate HOT Stem (e.g. *who, what, where, when*).

5. List these questions under the Factual section of the Cognitive Rigor Question Framework.

Figure 3.8   Good Factual Questions Generator

TASK	HIGHER-ORDER THINKING	HOT STEM	DOK CONTEXT
Vocabulary Knowledge	Define Describe Explain Identify Understand	What What does it mean?	
Close Reading	Recognize Read Review	Who What Where When	
Information Literacy	Research Retrieve Record Refer to	Who is/are What is/are Where is/are When does/did	

4

How Do Good Analytical Questions Deepen Knowledge and Thinking?

You are teaching a unit on forces and motion. Your students are expected to do the following:

- Apply Newton's Third Law to design a solution to a problem involving the motion of two colliding objects. (NGSS-MS-PS2-1)

- Plan an investigation to provide evidence that the change in an object's motion depends on the sum of the forces on the object and the mass of the object. (NGSS-MS-PS2-2)

- Ask questions about data to determine the factors that affect the strength of electric and magnetic forces. (NGSS-MS-PS2-3)

- Present arguments using constructed evidence to support the claim that gravitational interactions are attractive and depend on the masses of interacting objects. (NGSS-MS-PS2-4)

- Conduct an investigation and evaluate the experimental design to provide evidence that fields exist between objects exerting forces on each other even though the objects are not in contact. (NGSS-MS-PS2-5)

The students will respond to the good analytical questions outlined in Figure 4.1.

Notice how deeply the performance objectives of this lesson prompt students to communicate their learning by developing models, conducting investigations, and constructing cogent arguments. Before students share the results of their work, however, they need to develop a deeper conceptual understanding about the different types of forces and interactions that influence motion and stability.

Figure 4.1   Good Analytical Questions: Forces and Motion

ANALYTICAL	**How and why can an object's continued motion, its change in motion, or its stability be predicted?***
	• How can Newton's Third Law be used to solve a problem involving the motion between two colliding objects?
	• Why does the change in an object's motion depend upon the sum of the gravitational forces on the object and its mass?
	• How can the strength of electric and magnetic forces be determined?
	• Why do gravitational interactions create attraction and how do these interactions depend upon the masses of the interacting objects?
	• How can fields exist between objects exerting gravitational forces on each other even though the objects are not in contact?
	* May also be used as a topical essential question.

Now look at the good questions derived from the standards in Figure 4.1. Notice how they promote cognitive rigor by expanding students' thinking from basic who, what, where, and when inquiry to questions that promote deeper understanding—how and why can an object's continued or change in motion or stability be explained. These questions also move students from acquiring information they need to know or understand to deeper questions that explain different natural events and phenomena. That's a big step in the learning process, and that's the intent of good analytical questions.

What Good Analytical Questions Do

Good analytical questions teach students to think—not what or how to think, but to think deeply about the content they are learning. These questions focus on cognition and allow students to process this information into disciplinary knowledge (or the ability to respond as professionals or specialists do).

Analytical questions and the cognitive rigor they promote prompt students to do the following:

• **Examine** what is the meaning or message; what is the intent or purpose; and what is inferred, implied, or symbolized.

• **Experiment with** how or why a concept or process can be used to answer questions, address problems, and accomplish tasks.

• **Explain** what categorizes, characterizes, or classifies an idea, incident, individual, or issue based upon certain criteria.

These are the required cognitive deep thinking processes needed for college and career readiness in the 21st century. These deep thinking skills engage students in examining the meaning behind data, definitions, details, facts, and formulas. They also encourage students to understand the intent of texts and analyze inferences. Responses to good analytical questions, as opposed to responses to basic factual questions, strengthen students' thinking abilities and move them toward using this deeper knowledge to investigate phenomena and solve problems. These good questions deepen students' knowledge and understanding in the following areas.

Content Knowledge and Conceptual Understanding

One of the key objectives of cognitive rigor is for students to process the vast amount of information they have acquired into deeper knowledge and thinking that is both understandable and manageable. Asking good analytical questions is critical to the process because these questions prompt students to "see the larger constructs inherent in the information and the relationships between ideas and attendant concepts and theories" (Conley, 2005). By responding to analytical questions, students will develop and demonstrate the following:

• **Content knowledge** to explain scenarios through categorization, classification, generalization, and use of principles, models, and theories (i.e., how information can be processed into knowledge and thinking).

• **Conceptual understanding** or how and why the facts and figures can be used to discover the meaning and significance behind data, definitions, details, and stated fact.

Analytical questions prompt students to explore how and why different models and theories can be used "to present a clear, rounded, and systemic view of a complex phenomenon, problem, or subject matter" (Anderson & Krathwohl, 2001, p. 51). Students are also encouraged to question the meaning and thinking underlying the concepts and content they are learning. Good analytical questions (Figure 4.2) challenge students to show and tell content knowledge and conceptual understanding.

Procedural and Transferable Knowledge

Procedural knowledge is what Anderson and Krathwohl (2001) define as the knowledge of how to do something from the subject- and criteria-specific algorithms, formulas, and methods the students are working with. The learning goals associated with cognitive rigor demand a level of learning beyond knowing and

Figure 4.2   Good Factual Questions Versus Good Analytical Questions

GOOD FACTUAL QUESTIONS	GOOD ANALYTICAL QUESTIONS
What is Edgar Allan Poe's philosophy of composition?	How does Edgar Allan Poe convey his philosophy of composition in his own works?
What is modernism?	How does modernism reflect the ideas and ideals of late 19th and early 20th century Western society through art and literature?
What is the alphabetic principle?	How can the alphabetic principle explain how spoken words are represented in written language by specific sequences of letters?
What are the properties of equality?	How do the properties of equality determine the equivalence of equations?
What is lattice mathematics?	How can lattice mathematics be used to determine the product of multi-digit numbers?
What are the laws of physics?	How can the laws of physics explain natural occurrences and phenomena?
What is Newton's Second Law of Motion?	How does Newton's Second Law of Motion govern the motion of an object that is subjected to forces?
What is Darwin's Theory of Evolution?	How does the biological evolutionary model based on Darwin's theory explain how existing species arise from earlier species through the mechanism of natural selection?
What is the Punnett Square?	How does the Punnett Square show and predict genetic patterns and probabilities?
What is collision theory?	How does collision theory provide a qualitative model for explaining the rates of chemical reactions?
What is the Periodic Table?	How does the Periodic Table classify chemical elements based upon the following criteria? • Atomic number • Electron configurations • Chemical properties
What is Ohm's Law?	How does Ohm's Law explain why the current that passes through a conductor between two points is directly proportional to the potential difference across the two points?
What are the various attributes of a monarchy?	What distinguishes the various attributes of a monarchy?
What are the various ideologies of democracy?	How have other ideologies of democracy been adopted by different nations?
What is the law of supply and demand?	How does the law of supply and demand explain price determination in a market?

showing *how* to use procedures to analyzing and telling *why* procedures are used in various circumstances and contexts. That is what is meant by the need to develop transferable knowledge. Knowing and demonstrating how to use procedures, however, is half the battle. Cognitive rigor also expects students to examine, experiment with, and explain *how and why* different procedures can be used to attain a particular answer, outcome, or result. The deeper analysis and in-depth explanation of procedures will help students develop both transferable knowledge and personal expertise in a particular area or subject.

Figure 4.2 demonstrates the cognitive rigor differences between factual questions and analytical questions focused on deepening procedural understanding.

Notice how the factual questions in Figure 4.2 require students to describe the procedure specifically. The majority of these questions would be designated as a DOK-2 or DOK-3 depending upon the detail required for the response. For example, are students expected to explain how to use the procedure (DOK-2) or to explain how the procedure can be used (DOK-3)? The interpretation of the question depends upon the context and the extent of the required response.

Analytical questions also prompt students to think strategically how and why procedures can be used to provide a specific answer or result. Consider how the following scenario engages students to communicate procedural knowledge as they solve math problems using place value and the properties of operations.

You are teaching a unit on using place value understanding and properties of operations to perform multidigit arithmetic. Your students are expected to demonstrate or communicate the following:

- Confidently add and subtract multi-digit whole numbers using the standard algorithm. (CCSS.MATH.CONTENT.4.NBT.B.4)

- Multiply a whole number of up to four digits by a one-digit whole number, and multiply two two-digit numbers, using strategies based on place value and the properties of operations. Illustrate and explain the calculation by using equations, rectangular arrays, and/or area models. (CCSS.MATH.CONTENT.4.NBT.B.5)

- Find whole-number quotients and remainders with up to four-digit dividends and one-digit divisors, using strategies based on place value, the properties of operations, and/or the relationship between multiplication and division. Illustrate and explain the calculation by using equations, rectangular arrays, and/or area models. (CCSS.MATH.CONTENT.4.NBT.B.6)

Your students will respond to the good questions in Figure 4.3.

Figure 4.3   Good Analytical Questions: Multidigit Arithmetic

ANALYTICAL	**How can understanding place value and properties of operations be used to perform multidigit arithmetic?*** • How can multidigit whole numbers be added and subtracted using the standard algorithm? • How can a whole number of up to four digits be multiplied by a one-digit whole number using strategies based upon place value and the properties of operations? • How can two two-digit numbers be multiplied using strategies based upon place value and the properties of operations? • How can whole-number quotients and remainders with up to four-digit dividends and one-digit divisors be found using the following? - Strategies based on place value - The properties of operations - The relationship between multiplication and division • How can calculations be illustrated and explained using the following? - Equations - Rectangular arrays - Area models * May also be used as a topical essential question.

Consider the expectations for this lesson and the expectation for students to think beyond demonstrating the procedural knowledge required to solve the problems. The students must answer the question *how*. As such, the topical essential question for this lesson requires students to explain place value and properties of operations and then to explain how these mathematical concepts can be used to perform multidigit arithmetic. The performance objectives of the individual standards engage students to explain how calculations can be performed using equations, rectangular arrays, and/or area models. This is the deep and transferable knowledge students must communicate, therefore the specific curriculum used in class must support their responses.

Authentic Literacy

In Chapter 3, we discussed how good factual questions engage students to closely review texts to identify essential information and to encourage critical thinking by doing the following:

- **Summarize** what the text means and what its message is.
- **Explain** what the intent or purpose of the text is.
- **Determine** what the text and its individual parts infer or suggest.

• **Deconstruct** how and why the text and author convey ideas and information (McConachie et al., 2006; Schmoker, 2011; Vacca, 2002).

These are the required cognitive actions associated with authentic literacy which Schmoker (2011) defines as deeper and purposeful reading, writing, thinking, and discussion about what students are learning. Authentic literacy encourages students to think beyond what the text says and to focus more on analyzing what and how and the manner in which the text is presented. Consider how the following good analytical questions engage students to think critically about the principles articulated in the Declaration of Independence.

You are teaching about the principles and purpose of the Declaration of Independence. Your students are expected to communicate and demonstrate the following:

- Understand the principles articulated in the Declaration of Independence. (NHS. USE3.1.B)

- Infer the intended audience and purpose of a historical source from information within the source itself and critique the usefulness of historical sources for a specific historical inquiry based on their maker, date, place of origin, and purpose. (C3. D2.His.9.3-12)

- Read closely to determine what the text says explicitly and to make logical inferences from it; cite specific textual evidence when writing or speaking to support conclusions drawn from the text. (CCSS.ELA-LITERACY.CCRA.R.1)

- Analyze the structure of texts, including how specific sentences, paragraphs, and larger portions of the text (e.g., a section, chapter, scene, or stanza) relate to each other and the whole. (CCSS.ELA-LITERACY.CCRA.R.5)

- Evaluate the argument and specific claims in a text, including the validity of the reasoning and the relevance and sufficiency of the evidence. (CCSS.ELA-LITERACY. CCRA.R.8)

- Write informative/explanatory texts to examine and convey complex ideas and information clearly and accurately through the effective selection, organization, and analysis of content. (CCSS.ELA-LITERACY.CCRA.W.2)

- Draw evidence from literary or informational texts to support analysis, reflection, and research. (CCSS.ELA-LITERACY.CCRA.W.9)

- Apply knowledge of language to understand how language functions in different contexts, to make effective choices for meaning or style, and to comprehend more fully when reading or listening. (CCSS.ELA-LITERACY.CCRA.L.3)

The students will address the analytical questions in Figure 4.4.

Figure 4.4   Good Analytical Questions: The Declaration of Independence

ANALYTICAL	**How does the Declaration of Independence express the grievances of the colonists?***
	• What is the intent of the Declaration of Independence?
	• What are the meaning and message of the Declaration of Independence?
	• What does the Declaration of Independence represent?
	• How does the Declaration of Independence address the following themes: freedom, independence, tyranny, democracy, unalienable rights?
	• How is the style and tone of the Declaration of Independence idealistic, legalistic, and practical?
	• How does the crafting and structure of the Declaration of Independence strengthen its message and purpose?
	• How does the Declaration of Independence incorporate different conventions of craft, structure, writing, and language to convey its intent and purpose?
	• How did the colonists emphasize their concerns in the Declaration of Independence?
	• How and why is the Declaration of Independence written like a formal legal document?
	• What can be inferred from the opening "The Unanimous Declaration of the thirteen United States of America"?
	• What does this statement mean or infer? *"We hold these truths to be self-evident, that all men are created equal, that they are endowed by their Creator with certain unalienable rights, that among these are life, liberty and the pursuit of happiness."*
	• What does the Declaration of Independence infer by calling rights "unalienable"?
	• Why does the Declaration of Independence refer directly to the "present King of Great Britain" and begin every one of their complaints by referring to what "he" has done instead of referring to the nation of Great Britain and its people?
	• Why has this document continued to remain relevant and timeless historically and presently?
	* May also be used as a topical essential question.

This lesson does not ask students to demonstrate basic understanding of what is the Declaration of Independence. The goal is for students to analyze the intent of this historical document and share their perspective on the document's meaning and message. By addressing these analytical questions, students are challenged to read the text closely and to make logical inferences from it.

Good analytical questions also engage students to participate in deeper analysis and discussion of the central ideas and themes of a text and how authors craft and structure texts to present their perspective. Consider how the following good analytical questions engage students in a literary analysis of the central ideas and themes addressed in a particular work of literary fiction.

You are teaching a book study on *The Scarlet Letter* by Nathaniel Hawthorne. Your students are expected to do the following:

- Determine central ideas or themes of a text and analyze their development; summarize the key supporting details and ideas. (CCSS.ELA-LITERACY.CCRA.R.2)

- Analyze how and why individuals, events, or ideas develop and interact over the course of the text. (CCSS.ELA-LITERACY.CCRA.R.3)

- Assess how point of view or purpose shapes the content and style of the text. (CCSS.ELA-LITERACY.CCRA.R.6)

- Analyze how two or more texts address similar themes or topics in order to build knowledge or to compare the approaches the authors take. (CCSS.ELA-LITERACY.CCRA.R.9)

- Write informative/explanatory texts to examine and convey complex ideas and information clearly and accurately through the effective selection, organization, and analysis of content. (CCSS.ELA-LITERACY.CCRA.W.2)

The students will address the good questions in Figure 4.5.

Notice how these analytical questions prompt students to look beyond who, what, where, or when and to think critically about how the text addresses certain ideas and themes. The questions also stimulate students to think about the meaning of the text and what the author suggests—in this case, Hawthorne's criticisms of Puritan culture. By responding to good analytical questions, students are encouraged to understand a text's central ideas and themes, as well as how the structure of the text conveys the author's perspective directly and indirectly.

How Do We Teach with Good Analytical Questions?

Good analytical questions can also be used as the essential question to set the instructional focus of a lesson's or unit's summative assessment. These questions are directly derived from the performance objectives of college- and career-ready standards and are why the overarching topical questions ask how and why. (Chapter 2 explained in detail the relationship between good essential and analytical questions.)

Let's take a look at how analytical questions set the instructional focus and serve as the summative assessment in each of the content areas.

Figure 4.5   Good Analytical Questions: *The Scarlet Letter*
by Nathaniel Hawthorne

ANALYTICAL	**How does *The Scarlet Letter* embody the common motifs, style, and themes of individualism and romanticism and also serve as a criticism of the beliefs and ideals of Puritanism?***
	• How does the author express his perspective about Puritan culture and society in *The Scarlet Letter*?
	• How does *The Scarlet Letter* address the themes of guilt, blame, and sin and how it is perceived stereotypically, religiously, psychologically, and socially through the four main characters in the novel?*
	• What does Nathaniel Hawthorne infer about the flaws and hypocrisy of Puritan culture in *The Scarlet Letter*?
	• What does the scarlet letter represent?
	• How does its symbolic meaning change over the course of the novel?
	• How does Nathaniel Hawthorne use the symbol of the scarlet letter with his four main characters to criticize the Puritan world and to question whether their beliefs and punishments are justified?
	• How does Nathaniel Hawthorne convey the role and treatment of women in the Puritan world in this book?
	• Why is Nathaniel Hawthorne's representation of the Puritans and their culture in *The Scarlet Letter* both an observation and a criticism?
	• What is the purpose of the opening Custom-House essay at the beginning of the novel?
	* May also be used as a topical essential question.

English Language Arts, Fine Arts, Visual Arts

Good analytical questions transition students from recognizing the key ideas and details of a text to understanding and analyzing the following:

- How and why do ideas, individuals, and information develop?
- How and why can texts be crafted and structured?
- How and why can knowledge and ideas be integrated and presented?

These are the good questions that measure teaching for cognitive rigor in literature and the arts. The questions encourage students to critically consider works they are reading and to think about how the authors achieve certain audience responses. Good analytical questions extend student comprehension to include the following inquiries:

- How does a text address a central idea or theme?
- What is the intent and purpose of the text?

• What is the perspective or point of view of a text?

• What inferences can be made from the key details and ideas presented in the text?

Good analytical questions also challenge students to think critically about the following:

• How do texts use the conventions of language and writing to support the writer's perspective, point of view, and purpose?

• How do texts build, integrate, and present knowledge and ideas using diverse media and formats?

• How can texts be presented, produced, and published clearly, comprehensively, and creatively?

Mathematics

In mathematics, good analytical questions engage students to think deeply about how and why mathematics can be used to answer questions, address problems, and accomplish tasks. These good questions shift the focus of instruction and learning from doing math to explaining how and why problems can be solved by applying mathematical facts, concepts, operations, and procedures. Consider the following deep mathematical learning experience:

You are teaching a unit on extending previous understandings of multiplication and division to include dividing by fractions. Your students will do the following:

• Interpret and compute quotients of fractions, and solve word problems involving division of fractions by fractions, (e.g., by using visual fraction models and equations to represent the problem). (CCSS.MATH.CONTENT.6.NS.A.1)

Your students will address and respond to the questions in Figure 4.6 using the mathematical problems as textual evidence to support their responses.

The good analytical questions in Figure 4.6 encourage students to delve deeper into the math they are learning and communicate how their previous knowledge of multiplication and division can be applied to the division of fractions. This requirement sets the instructional focus and serves as the summative assessment. Over the course of the unit, students examine the meaning of the rule $(a/b) \div (c/d) = ad/bc$ and how word problems that involve division of fractions by fractions can be solved using visual fraction models and equations to represent the problem.

Figure 4.6   Good Analytical Questions: Fractions

	How can two different fractions be equal and have equivalent values even though they have different denominators?*
ANALYTICAL	• What does it mean when fraction a/b is stated to be equivalent to a fraction $(n \times a) / (n \times b)$?
	• How can two fractions with different numerators and denominators be compared by creating common denominators or numerators?
	• How can two fractions with different numerators and denominators be compared using benchmark fractions?
	• Why are comparisons between fractions valid only when the two fractions refer to the same whole?
	• How can the results of comparisons be recorded with symbols >, =, or <?
	• How can the results of comparisons and conclusions be validated and verified using visual fraction models?
	* May also be used as a topical essential question.

Students still need to prove they can do the math required to solve the problems; however, the problems serve as textual evidence to support their explanations of computing quotients of fractions and how this knowledge can be used to solve both mathematical and real-world problems no matter the circumstance or context. These good questions deepen the students' practical mathematical knowledge and build strategic understanding of how mathematical concepts, operations, and procedures can be used to explain answers and outcomes.

Science

Good analytical questions applied to science focus on how and why scientific models, principles, and theories can be used to study phenomena and solve problems in the natural world. Consider how the following good analytical questions engage students to examine wave patterns and properties.

You are teaching a unit on wave properties. Your students are expected to communicate or demonstrate the following:

• Develop a model of waves to describe patterns in terms of amplitude and wavelength and that waves can cause objects to move. (NGSS-4-PS4-1)

Your students will address the good questions in Figure 4.7.

Figure 4.7   Good Analytical Questions: Amplitude and Wavelength

ANALYTICAL	**How can waves be described in terms of amplitude and wavelength and cause objects to move?***
	• What characterizes the properties and behaviors of waves?
	• How can waves of the same type differ in amplitude (height of the wave) and wavelength (spacing between wave peaks)?
	• How are waves a repeating pattern of motion that transfers energy from place to place without overall displacement of matter?
	• Why does the wavelength and frequency of a wave depend on the medium in which the wave is traveling?
	• How and why can waves add to or cancel one another as they cross, depending on their relative phase (i.e., relative position of peaks and troughs of the waves)?
	• Why can waves emerge unaffected by each other as they cross?
	• How can waves be combined with other waves of the same type to produce complex information-containing patterns that can be decoded at the receiving end?
	• How do waves transfer energy and any encoded information without the bulk motion of matter?
	• How can waves travel unchanged over long distances, pass through other waves undisturbed, and be detected and decoded far from where they were produced?
	• How do the human ear and brain work together at detecting and decoding patterns of information in sound and distinguishing them from random noise?
	• How is resonance used in the design of all musical instruments and in the production of sound by the human voice?
	• Why is a wave not affected as much when it passes through an object that is small compared with its wavelength?
	• How can scientists and engineers design systems for transferring information across long distances, storing information, and investigating nature on many scales by understanding wave properties and the interactions of electromagnetic radiation with matter?
	* May also be used as a topical essential question.

Notice how the first question sets up the instructional focus and serves as the summative assessment for the unit. The following questions also ask students to examine how and why waves cause objects to move and to explain these wave patterns in terms of amplitude and wavelength. The subsequent analytical questions drive students' continued scientific examinations with wave patterns and properties. Responding to these good questions promotes a deeper understanding of these principles and supports the transfer and use of that knowledge.

Conclusion

Good analytical questions truly embody the concept of cognitive rigor because they challenge students to understand and analyze *how and why*. They also expect students not only to know and show but also to analyze and tell *how and why concepts and procedures can be used* to answer questions, address problems, and accomplish tasks. Addressing and responding to these questions will deepen students' understanding about concepts and content. This will also help students develop both transferable knowledge and personal expertise they can use to answer *any* question, address *any* problem, accomplish *any* task, or analyze *any* text or topic that correlates to the concepts and content they are learning. Keep in mind that it's not only the question stem that promotes cognitive rigor but how strategically and extensively students are encouraged to examine and explain concepts and content.

PROFESSIONAL DEVELOPMENT
How to Develop Good Analytical Questions to Deepen Knowledge and Thinking

Objective

Develop good analytical questions from the performance objectives of college- and career-ready standards that challenge students to think deeply about the texts or topics they are reviewing.

This is an extension of the professional development from Chapter 2 that focuses on developing good essential questions.

Materials

- College- and career-ready standards adopted by your state
- Curriculum and texts adopted by your school
- Good Questions and Bloom's Taxonomy (Figure 1.2)
- Good Questions and Depth of Knowledge (Figure 1.4)

Procedure

1. Identify the academic standards, texts, and topics that will be addressed as part of the lesson or unit.

2. Determine the cognitive action the student is expected to demonstrate. Select the HOT Stem that addresses this cognitive demand.

3. Describe the concept or procedure that will be examined, experimented with, and explained. Record it after the HOT Stem in Figure 4.8.

4. Choose which question will set the instructional focus and serve as the summative assessment for the lesson or unit. Make this question the topical essential question for the unit. Use the other questions derived from the standards as the supplemental cognitive rigor questions that will be addressed within the unit.

a. Math: Rephrase the bold cluster as a good analytical question that will set the instructional focus and serve as the summative assessment for the unit. This will be the topical essential question for the unit. Rephrase the standards under the cluster into good analytical questions that set the instructional focus and serve as summative assessments for individual lessons within the unit.

b. English Language Arts: Choose one of the standards listed under the Key Ideas and Details strand that will set the instructional focus and serve as the summative assessment. Rephrase the performance objective into a good analytical question that specifically addresses the literary or informational text being read and reviewed. Turn the other reading standards into good analytical questions that will engage students as they closely read and authentically respond to the text.

c. Science: Rephrase the performance objective of the college- and career-ready standards into good analytical questions that engage students to examine, explain, and experiment with the scientific concepts and practices addressed in the standard. (Note: Next Generation Science Standards include good analytical questions that can serve as good topic questions for a unit.)

d. History/Social Studies: Rephrase the bold cluster as a good analytical question that will set the instructional focus and serve as the summative assessment. Turn the standards under the cluster into good analytical questions that set the instructional focus and serve as summative assessments for individual lessons within the unit.

e. Fine Arts/Visual Arts: Rephrase the performance objective of the college- and career-ready standards for responding and connecting into good analytical questions that specifically address the literary or informational text being read and reviewed. Choose one of the good analytical questions to set instructional purpose and serve as the summative assessment for reading and reviewing the assigned text. Turn the other standards into good analytical questions that will engage students to closely read and authentically respond to the visual, dramatic, or musical performances and productions.

Figure 4.8   Good Analytical Questions Generator

EXAMINE EXPERIMENT WITH EXPLAIN	How			
	Why			
PROCEDURAL KNOWLEDGE	How does		work to	
	How can		be used to	
	Why does		work to	
	Why can		be used to	
CONCEPTUAL KNOWLEDGE	What categorizes			
	What characterizes			
	What classifies			
	What distinguishes			
	What indicates			
	What are the similarities			
	What are the differences			
AUTHENTIC LITERACY	What is the intent			
	What is the purpose			
	What does the text infer			
	What is the meaning			
	What is the message			
	What does			represent?
	What does the author suggest			
	What does			symbolize?
	What is the tone			
	What is the author's purpose			

5

How Do Good Reflective Questions Expand Knowledge and Thinking?

You are teaching a unit on the sources and character of cultural, religious, and social reform movements in the antebellum period of the United States. Your students are expected to demonstrate and communicate the following:

- Understand how Americans strived to reform society and create a distinct culture. (NHS.USE3.4.B)

- Determine central ideas or themes of a text and analyze their development; summarize the key supporting details and ideas. (CCSS.ELA-LITERACY.CCRA.R.2)

- Assess how point of view or purpose shapes the content and style of a text. (CCSS. ELA-LITERACY.CCRA.R.6)

- Analyze how two or more texts address similar themes or topics in order to build knowledge or to compare the approaches the authors take. (CCSS.ELA-LITERACY. CCRA.R.9)

- Write informative/explanatory texts to examine and convey complex ideas and information clearly and accurately through the effective selection, organization, and analysis of content. (CCSS.ELA-LITERACY.CCRA.W.2)

- Conduct short as well as more sustained research projects based on focused questions, demonstrating understanding of the subject under investigation. (CCSS. ELA-LITERACY.CCRA.W.7)

- Draw evidence from literary or informational texts to support analysis, reflection, and research. (CCSS.ELA-LITERACY.CCRA.W.9)

Your students will respond to the good questions outlined in Figure 5.1.

Figure 5.1   Good Reflective Questions: 19th Century U.S. History

REFLECTIVE	• What is the connection between history and literacy?
	• What influence did the Second Great Awakening and the ideas of its principal leaders have on the following aspects of U.S. society and culture?
	  - Politics
	  - Ideals
	  - Philosophy
	  - Art and literature
	• What influence did the Second Great Awakening have on the following?
	  - Transcendentalism
	  - Public education
	  - Women's suffrage
	  - Abolition
	  - Commercialism
	• What caused the rise of transcendentalism in the early 19th century?
	• What influence did the Puritans have on the transcendentalist movement?
	• What caused the American Renaissance?
	• What were the reasons and results of the utopian experiments in the early 19th century?
	• What caused the end of the transcendentalist movement?
	• What was the relationship between Ralph Waldo Emerson and Henry David Thoreau, and what influence did they have on each other and the transcendentalist movement?
	• What is the connection between transcendentalism and idealism according to Emerson?
	• What are the reasons for Thoreau's rejection of materialism and conformity in *Walden*?
	• What past and current influences have the writings of Emerson and Thoreau had on individuals, society, and culture?

The instructional focus of this unit is on the origins and character of cultural, religious, and social reform movements in the antebellum period of the United States. Students are challenged to examine how the writings of two key leaders in transcendentalism, Ralph Waldo Emerson and Henry David Thoreau, affected and underpinned U.S. society and culture and the Second Great Awakening.

Note how the good reflective questions for this lesson prompt students to expand their thinking about the relationship between history and literature and to explore universal, essential questions beyond traditional K–12 education. Cognitive rigor is also supported since these questions require students to think deeply about how they can use what they learn to strengthen their thinking, address problems, and accomplish tasks.

What Good Reflective Questions Do

Good reflective questions teach students to analyze *why* and encourage them to be evaluative and reflective as they do the following:

- **Inquire** about why knowledge can be used to study phenomena and solve problems.
- **Investigate** causes, connections, and consequences.

These are the cognitive processes that involve a combination of planning, reasoning, and higher-order thinking processes outlined by both Bloom and Webb (Hess, 2013). They are called reflective because they ask students not only to analyze but also to evaluate why—or rather, to explore and reflect upon what are the reasons behind relationships and results. They also encourage students to delve even deeper by going beyond the teacher, the text, and even the topic as it's presented. When students are provided the opportunity to extend their thinking, it not only broadens their understanding but also challenges them to synthesize their education and experiences into expertise.

The goal of good reflective questions is to prompt students to come up with as much evidence and as many examples as possible to expand their knowledge and thinking. Consider how the good reflective questions in Figure 5.2 provide students the opportunity to conduct deeper investigations into the texts and topics they are reading in class.

Notice how the performance objectives in Figure 5.2 limit students to identifying or listing certain responses and how good reflective questions prompt students to explore these topics in depth. Reflective questions expand students' knowledge and thinking by requiring them to reflect upon reasons, relationships, causes, connections, and consequences.

Reflective questions associated with cognitive rigor are more about expanding and expressing depth of knowledge. Factual questions require students to focus on acquiring factual knowledge. Analytical questions require students to develop and demonstrate conceptual and procedural knowledge. Reflective questions expand knowledge and extend thinking to study phenomena, solve problems, and think strategically and extensively about *why*—or rather, *what are the reasons, relationships, results, and ramifications*. Let's take a look at how good reflective questions help students extend their knowledge and thinking about the texts and topics they are reading.

Figure 5.2   Making Good Reflective Questions from Performance Objectives

SPECIFIC PERFORMANCE OBJECTIVES	GOOD REFLECTIVE QUESTIONS
List 3 reasons why Mark Twain chose to write *The Adventures of Huckleberry Finn* as a satire.	What are the reasons that Mark Twain chose to write *The Adventures of Huckleberry Finn* as a satire?
Identify 4 ways the quotient of two numbers divided by each other can be determined.	What are the ways the quotient of two numbers divided by each other can be determined?
Identify 5 reasons water is important for life on Earth.	What are the reasons life on Earth is so dependent on water?
Identify 6 ways to prevent or reduce deforestation.	What are the ways deforestation can be prevented or reduced?
List 7 causes of the Great Depression.	What caused the Great Depression?
Identify 8 causes of pollution.	What causes pollution?
List 9 effects alcohol has on the body.	What effect does alcohol have on the body?
Identify 10 ways new media and technology are changing people, society, and cultures politically, socially, economically, professionally, geographically, and academically.	What influence has new media and technology had on people, cultures, and society in the following areas? • Historically • Politically • Socially • Economically • Professionally • Geographically • Academically

Strategic Knowledge

Reflective questions that address strategic knowledge focus on explaining *why*—that is, why is this the answer, why is this the outcome, why is this the result. These questions expand upon analytical questions that address conceptual and procedural knowledge by focusing students on *why* information should be used instead of *how*. In this context, *why* is more evaluative since students are required to clarify the reasons behind their answers. Consider how the following scenario engages students to think strategically about why outcomes and results can be explained with mathematical functions.

You are teaching a unit on defining, evaluating, and comparing functions. Your students are expected to do the following:

- Understand that a function is a rule that assigns to each input exactly one output. The graph of a function is the set of ordered pairs consisting of an input and the corresponding output. (CCSS.MATH.CONTENT.8.F.A.1)

- Compare properties of two functions each represented in a different way (algebraically, graphically, numerically in tables, or by verbal descriptions). (CCSS.MATH. CONTENT.8.F.A.2)

- Interpret the equation $y = mx + b$ as defining a linear function, whose graph is a straight line; give examples of functions that are not linear. (CCSS. MATH.CONTENT.8.F.A.3)

Your students will address and respond to the good questions outlined in Figure 5.3.

Figure 5.3   Good Reflective Questions: Functions

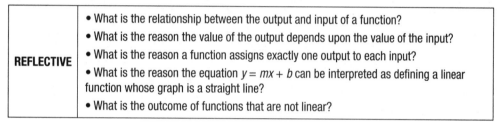

REFLECTIVE	• What is the relationship between the output and input of a function? • What is the reason the value of the output depends upon the value of the input? • What is the reason a function assigns exactly one output to each input? • What is the reason the equation $y = mx + b$ can be interpreted as defining a linear function whose graph is a straight line? • What is the outcome of functions that are not linear?

Take a close look at the standards in Figure 5.3. For the most part, the expectations are explicit. However, they do prompt and encourage students to question *why*—or rather, what is the reason. Understanding the rule of function involves understanding *what is the reason*. Comparing properties of functions represented in different ways and interpreting the equations as linear and nonlinear and giving examples of them engage students to clarify *what is the reason*. Consider part of the first standard, *"The graph of a function is the set of ordered pairs consisting of an input and the corresponding output."* It asks students to question and explore *why* or *what is the reason*. Reflective questions ask students to think strategically and use reasoning to clarify why a practice, principle, or process can be used to produce a certain answer, desired outcome, or specific result.

Reflective questions that are focused on reasons can also expand students' knowledge and thinking beyond stated learning goals and performance objectives. For example, math performance objectives often challenge students to do the math but expect them to explore the fundamental question of why certain results are achieved. Asking reflective questions accomplishes this result.

Deep Knowledge

Reflective questions move students from researching who, what, where, and when to investigating the cause, effect, influence, and results, all focused on gaining deep knowledge that can be used in multiple contexts (Walkup & Jones, 2014). Consider how the following reflective questions expand students' knowledge about cultural transformations that occurred in Western Europe during the Renaissance.

You are teaching a unit on the Renaissance. Your students are expected to do the following:

- Analyze the social and intellectual significance of the technological innovation of printing with movable type. (NHS.WHE6.2.B.1)

- Explain connections between the Italian Renaissance and the development of humanist ideas in Europe north of the Alps. (NHS.WHE6.2.B.2)

- Evaluate major achievements in literature, music, painting, sculpture, and architecture in 16th-century Europe. (NHS.WHE6.2.B.3)

- Explain connections between the Scientific Revolution and its antecedents such as Greek rationalism, medieval theology, Muslim science, Renaissance humanism, and new global knowledge. (NHS.WHE6.2.D.1)

- Explain connections between the Enlightenment and its antecedents such as Roman republicanism, the Renaissance, and the scientific revolution. (NHS.WHE6.2.E.1)

Your students will address and respond to the good questions in Figure 5.4.

Reflective questions also prompt and encourage students to explore and evaluate the connection between concepts and content within the specific subject area and across the curriculum. They guide students to explore *why* or *what is the reason* the concepts and content they are learning in one academic subject can be used to address and respond to different academic and real-world circumstances, issues, problems, and situations.

Relevant Knowledge

Reflective questions extend students' perspectives beyond the curriculum and classroom and ask them to demonstrate the following:

• **Global Awareness:** Knowledge and understanding of ideas, incidents, individuals, and issues on a more global scale and how to decisively, practically, and sensitively address them.

Figure 5.4   Good Reflective Questions: The Renaissance

REFLECTIVE	• What are the past and current global effects of the Renaissance?
	• What causes people, societies, and cultures to change?
	• What is the connection between the Italian Renaissance and the development of humanist ideas in Europe north of the Alps?
	• What impact and influence did the major achievements of the Renaissance have on the following?
	  - Science
	  - Literature
	  - Music
	  - Painting
	  - Sculpture
	  - Architecture
	• What is the connection between the Renaissance, the Scientific Revolution, and the Enlightenment?
	• What influence did the technological innovation of printing with movable type have on Western Europe socially and intellectually?

• **Financial Literacy:** Knowledge and understanding of the economy's role in society and how to make the best personal and professional choices.

• **Civic Literacy:** Knowledge and understanding of the role of the government in society and how to participate and make well-informed civic decisions.

• **Health Literacy:** Knowledge and understanding of national and international public health and safety issues and how to make the best preventive health-related decisions.

• **Environmental Literacy:** Knowledge and understanding of the environment and how to address environmental challenges appropriately.

• **Digital Media Literacy:** Broader knowledge and understanding of available digital resources and how to access, evaluate, and use these technologies (Partnership for 21st Century Learning, 2015; Trilling & Fadel, 2009).

These are considered to be "interdisciplinary 21st century themes relevant to some of the key issues and problems of our times" (Trilling & Fadel, 2009, p. 83). Reflective questions incorporate these themes to help students establish the relevance of the texts and topics being taught in school. They ask students to evaluate the connection, impact, influence, and relationship between ideas and information on a much grander scale.

Reflective questions also help make abstract concepts more concrete and extend the thinking of students in ways never considered. Think about how the following scenario prompts students to investigate the impact of natural disasters.

You are teaching a unit on natural hazards. Your students are expected to do the following:

- Analyze and interpret data on natural hazards to forecast future catastrophic events and inform the development of technologies to mitigate their effects. (NGSS-MS-ESS3-2)

- Apply scientific principles to design a method for monitoring and minimizing a human impact on the environment. (NGSS-MS-ESS3-3)

- Ask questions to clarify evidence of the factors that have caused the rise in global temperatures over the past century. (NGSS-MS-ESS3-5)

Your students are expected to address and respond to the good questions in Figure 5.5.

Figure 5.5   Natural Hazards

REFLECTIVE	• What are the causes and effects of a natural disaster? • What are the reasons that natural disasters are considered random and not random? • What is the connection between natural disasters and human activity? • What are the reasons that natural disasters cannot be predicted precisely? • What are the reasons people still settle in areas prone to natural disasters? • What influence have natural disasters had on developments in science, engineering, and technology in the past and today? • What is the connection between natural disasters and global climate change? • What has caused the rise in global temperatures in the last century? • What has been the effect of the rise in global temperatures over the past century?

Notice how these reflective questions serve to expand students' knowledge about natural hazards beyond academic perspectives and encourage them to explain different generalizations about connections between natural disasters and global warming.

How Can We Teach Using Good Reflective Questions?

As noted, reflective questions compel students to venture beyond the ideas and information presented by teachers or from the texts they read. Let's take a look at how good reflective questions help to expand student knowledge and thinking across a variety of the curriculum areas.

English Language Arts, Fine Arts, Visual Arts

Good reflective questions like those outlined in Figure 5.6, along with their factual and analytical counterparts, prompt students to expand their knowledge and thinking about what inspires writers, artists, and musicians to produce their works of literature, art, and music. By addressing these questions, students develop a much deeper understanding of the power of these texts and the unique way these creative people shared their perspective and point of view.

Mathematics

Reflective questions move students studying mathematics from experimenting with *how* math can be used to explore the reasons *why* math is used. The questions prompt students to analyze and prove their answers using top-down logic. Consider how the following scenario engages students to evaluate probability models using reasoning and proof.

You are teaching a lesson on investigating chance processes and the development, use, and evaluation of probability models. Your students are expected to do the following:

- Understand that the probability of a chance event is a number between 0 and 1 that expresses the likelihood of the event occurring. Larger numbers indicate greater likelihood. A probability near 0 indicates an unlikely event, a probability around 1/2 indicates an event that is neither unlikely nor likely, and a probability near 1 indicates a likely event. (CCSS.MATH.CONTENT.7.SP.C.5)

- Approximate the probability of a chance event by collecting data on the chance process that produces it and observing its long-run relative frequency, and predict the approximate relative frequency given the probability. (CCSS.MATH.CONTENT.7.SP.C.6)

- Develop a probability model and use it to find probabilities of events. Compare probabilities from a model to observed frequencies; if the agreement is not good, explain possible sources of the discrepancy. (CCSS.MATH.CONTENT.7.SP.C.7)

- Find probabilities of compound events using organized lists, tables, tree diagrams, and simulation. (CCSS.MATH.CONTENT.7.SP.C.8)

Figure 5.6   Factual, Analytical, and Reflective Questions: A Comparison

FACTUAL	ANALYTICAL	REFLECTIVE
• What is a trickster tale?	• How do the animal characters in trickster tales teach lessons about the following? - Folk wisdom - Human nature - Proper behavior	• What influence do trickster tales have on children's stories and cartoons featuring animals?
• What is mythology?	• How do mythological tales address the following themes: - Hero's journey and quest - Beauty - Love - Fate - War - Dangers of arrogance, ambition, hubris, and pride - Reward for goodness - Retribution for evil - Cannibalism	• What influence has the mythology of ancient cultures and societies had on modern storytelling and perspectives on life?
• Who is Edgar Allan Poe?	• How do Edgar Allan Poe's tales address the following themes? - Death - Love and hate - Self versus alter ego - Insanity versus rationality - Madness versus logic - Idealization of women - Obsession - Curiosity - Power of the dead over the living - Hope and despair - Animal instincts of humans	• What influence did Edgar Allan Poe's tales have on the following genres? - Detective mysteries - Horror - Science fiction - Poetry - Literary criticism
• What is Shakespearean drama?	• What characterizes a play as a Shakespearean comedy? • What characterizes a play as a Shakespearean tragedy?	• What influence have William Shakespeare's plays had on the following areas, historically and currently? - Drama - Art - Literature - Music - Behaviors and perspectives
• Who is Mark Twain?	• What distinguishes Mark Twain's writing style?	• What influence has Mark Twain had on satire and social criticism historically and presently?

• What is the plot of *The Great Gatsby* by F. Scott Fitzgerald? • What is the setting of *The Great Gatsby* by F. Scott Fitzgerald? • Who are the characters in *The Great Gatsby* by F. Scott Fitzgerald?	• How does *The Great Gatsby* address the following themes? - Society and class - Love - The American Dream - The Lost Generation - Wealth - Old money versus new money - Memory - Isolation - Mortality - Marriage and love	• What influenced F. Scott Fitzgerald to write *The Great Gatsby*? • What is the reason *The Great Gatsby* is considered be a social commentary on the following? - The corruption of the American Dream - Stratification of society - The Lost Generation - Materialism and wealth - Immorality and decadence
•What is dystopian science fiction? • What is censorship? • What is the plot of *Fahrenheit 451* by Ray Bradbury? • What is the plot of *1984* by George Orwell?	• What does Ray Bradbury suggest about censorship and privacy in *Fahrenheit 451*? • What does George Orwell infer about censorship and privacy in *1984*? • What are the similarities between how *Fahrenheit 451* and *1984* address issues of censorship and privacy?	• What is the reason *Fahrenheit 451* by Ray Bradbury and *1984* by George Orwell are examples of dystopian science fiction?
• Who is Leonardo da Vinci?	• How did Leonardo da Vinci design and produce the following paintings? - *Mona Lisa* - *The Last Supper* - *The Vitruvian Man*	• What influence did Leonardo da Vinci and his works have on the study of the following historically and presently? - Art - Architecture - Anatomy - Animals and botany - Mathematics - Science - Landscape and geology - Religion
• Who is Ludwig von Beethoven and what are his symphonies?	• What distinguished Beethoven's symphonies from one other?	• What effect does Beethoven and his symphonies have on musical composition and performance, both historically and today?
• What is a ballad? • What is lyric poetry?	• What categorizes a poem as a ballad? • What characterizes a poem as lyric poetry?	• What influence do ballads and lyric poems have on songwriting historically and presently?

Your students will address and respond to the good questions in Figure 5.7.

Figure 5.7   Good Reflective Questions: Probability

REFLECTIVE	• What are the reasons two or more outcomes in an event must be equally likely in order to determine theoretical probability?
	
	• What is the difference between theoretical probability and experimental probability?
	
	• What is the reason the theoretical probability of an event must be represented as a rational number between 0 and 1?
	
	• What is the reason for the theoretical probability of an event to be *certain* or *impossible*?
	
	• What is the reason larger numbers of probability indicate greater likelihood of an event occurring?
	
	• What are the reasons for the following?
	  - A probability near 0 indicates an unlikely event.
	  - A probability around 1/2 indicates an event that is neither unlikely nor likely.
	  - A probability near 1 indicates a likely event.
	
	• What is the reason the sum of the probability of an event and its complement is equal to 1 according to the algorithm P(event) + P(not event) = 1?
	
	• What is the reason the relative frequency of a chance event can be approximated given the probability?

Consider how students in these learning experiences are expected to examine how math is used to attain answers and investigate the reason probability models are used to clarify the results of events involving chance.

Reflective questions in mathematics are also helpful for teaching students how to answer test items that prompt them to analyze whether a problem was solved correctly. In essence, reflective questions promote mathematical thinking by shifting the instruction and assessment from explaining how a problem can be solved to clarifying why a solution is the right one. Such investigative strategies are also an excellent way to engage students in learning.

Science

Good reflective questions in science focus on establishing cause-and-effect and relationship patterns. The questions are used to prove that the effects observed or results recorded happened after the cause (Shuttleworth, 2009; Trochim, 2006). The performance objectives of science college- and career-ready standards are generally phrased to promote scientific inquiry through experimentation, argumentation, and engineering design.

Prior to developing and engaging in arguments, designs, and experiments, students can be encouraged to investigate the cause, connections, and consequences by responding to good reflective questions derived from these standards. To extend thinking with science topics, ask good reflective questions that prompt students to explore the effects of natural events on the different structures and systems of the world (e.g., geographical, political, economic, social), today and in the past.

History and Social Studies

Reflective questions in history and social studies also move students from researching the facts and how and why events occur to investigating the effects of current and past ideas, incidents, individuals, and issues. They also encourage students to expand their knowledge of history beyond what is presented to them or what they read on their own. Consider the following scenario about the consequences of the emergence of the first global age.

You are teaching a unit on how the transoceanic linking of the major world regions from 1450 to 1600 led to global transformations. Your students will demonstrate and communicate the following:

- Understand the origins and consequences of European overseas expansion in the 15th and 16th centuries. (NHS.WHE6.1.A)

- Understand the encounters between Europeans and peoples of Sub-Saharan Africa, Asia, and the Americas in the late 15th and early 16th centuries. (NHS.WHE6.1.B)

- Understand the consequences of the worldwide exchange of flora, fauna, and pathogens. (NHS.WHE6.1.C)

- Explain how the cultural and environmental characteristics of places change over time; analyze the combinations of cultural and environmental characteristics that make places both similar to and different from other places; evaluate how political and economic decisions throughout time have influenced cultural and environmental characteristics of various places and regions. (C3.D2.Geo.5.3-12)

- Describe how environmental and cultural characteristics influence population distribution in specific places or regions; and evaluate the impact of human settlement activities on the environmental and cultural characteristics of specific places and regions. (C3.D2.Geo.6.3-12)

- Analyze and explain how cultural and environmental characteristics affect the distribution and movement of people, goods, and ideas; how changes in transportation and communication technology influence the spatial connections among human settlements and affect the diffusion of ideas and cultural practices; analyze the reciprocal nature of how historical events and the spatial diffusion of ideas, technologies, and cultural practices have influenced migration patterns and the distribution of human population. (C3.D2.Geo.7.3-12)

Your students will address the good questions in Figure 5.8.

Figure 5.8   Good Reflective Questions: Geography

REFLECTIVE	• What were the causes and consequences of European overseas expansion in the 15th and 16th centuries?
	
	• What influence did the following have on European overseas expansion and conquests in the 15th and 16th centuries?
	  - Major social, economic, political, and cultural features of European society (Spain and Portugal in particular)
	  - Technological developments in shipbuilding, navigation, and naval warfare
	  - Motives, nature, and short-term significance of the major Iberian military
	  - Commercial expeditions to sub-Saharan Africa, Asia, and the Americas
	
	• What was the effect of the Portuguese maritime expansion to Africa, India, and Southeast Asia?
	
	• What was the relationship between the Portuguese and the people of Africa, India, and Southeast Asia?
	
	• What was the result of the Ottoman, Indian, Chinese, Japanese, Vietnamese, and Siamese (Thai) powers restricting European commercial, military, and political penetration?
	
	• What influence did the Catholic Church have in the foundation, organization, and administration of policies related to the indigenous populations of Spanish and Portuguese colonial empires in the Americas and Southeast Asia?
	
	• What were the consequences of the worldwide exchange of flora, fauna, and pathogens?
	
	• What effect did the exchange of plants and animals around the world in the late 15th and 16th centuries have on European, Asian, African, and Native American Indian societies and commerce?
	
	• What were the reasons the introduction of new disease microorganisms in the Americas after 1492 had such devastating demographic and social effects on Native American civilizations in North America and South America?
	
	• What effect did knowledge of the peoples, geography, and natural environment of the Americas have on European religious and intellectual life?

Notice how these reflective questions extend students' thinking by encouraging them to analyze the current and past effects of these events. With reflective history questions, the best way to encourage students to expand their knowledge and thinking is to ask students about the individual, societal, and cultural impact of these events, both in history and today. Asking these questions encourages students to explore the relevancy of these events as well as their causes, connections, and consequences.

Conclusion

Both reflective questions and analytical questions promote cognitive rigor by engaging students to analyze why. However, the depth of knowledge they ask students to share is different. Analytical questions focus primarily on prompting students to think deeply about how knowledge is used in a variety of circumstances; reflective questions ask students to expand their knowledge and think about why knowledge can be used to clarify answers, outcomes results, and solutions. These good questions complement each other, helping students build and develop the transferable and extensive knowledge they need to study phenomena and solve problems.

PROFESSIONAL DEVELOPMENT

How to Develop Good Reflective Questions to Expand Knowledge and Extend Thinking

Objective

Develop good reflective questions from the performance objectives of college- and career-ready standards that will encourage students to investigate the causes, connections, and consequences of events and experiences.

Materials
- College- and career-ready standards adopted by your state
- Curriculum and texts adopted by your school
- Good Questions and Bloom's Taxonomy (Figure 1.2)
- Good Questions and Depth of Knowledge (Figure 1.4)

Procedure

1. Identify the academic standards, texts, and topics that will be addressed as part of the lesson or unit. Use Figure 5.9 to record your work.

2. Determine whether the cognitive demand of the performance objective expects students to *analyze* or *evaluate*. Select the HOT Stem that addresses this cognitive demand.

a. For performance objectives that expect students to analyze why: Rephrase the performance objective into a reflective question that asks the student to investigate and inquire *what is the connection, the relationship, the outcome,* or *the result.*

b. For performance objectives that expect students to evaluate why: Rephrase the performance objective into a reflective question that asks the student to investigate and inquire *what effect, what influence,* and *what is the reason.*

Figure 5.9   Good Reflective Questions Generator

INVESTIGATE AND INQUIRE	What causes What caused	
	What is the connection	
	What is the relationship	
	What is the outcome	
	What is the result	
	What effect	
	What impact	
	What influence	
	What is the reason	

6

How Do Good Hypothetical Questions Pique Curiosity and Creativity?

You are teaching a unit on using place value and properties of operations to perform multidigit arithmetic. Your students are expected to do the following:

- Multiply a whole number of up to four digits by a one-digit whole number; multiply two two-digit numbers using strategies based on place value and the properties of operations. Illustrate the calculation and explain your work using equations, rectangular arrays, and area models. (CCSS.MATH.CONTENT.4.NBT.B.5)

The students will address and respond to the good questions in Figure 6.1.

So far we have discussed how factual questions help students build background knowledge and how analytical and reflective questions challenge students to think critically about *how* and *why* concepts and content can be used in a variety of contexts. Another aspect of cognitive rigor involves challenging students to think creatively by testing the boundaries of their knowledge and thinking—or rather, their imagination—by asking them to consider and confirm *what if*.

Note how good hypothetical questions in this unit on mathematics accomplish this shift in thinking—specifically, *how could* the different methods, models, strategies, and structures be used to solve multidigit multiplication problems. The context of these math problems challenges students to think strategically (DOK-3) and extend their thinking (DOK-4) about *how could* the mathematical concepts and procedures they are learning be transferred and used in both academic and real-world settings. By responding to these questions, students learn how to do math and also *envision and experiment with* about *how could* the math be applied in different contexts.

Figure 6.1   Good Hypothetical Questions: Multidigit Arithmetic

HYPOTHETICAL	• How could multidigit numbers be multiplied using the following methods? - Standard algorithm of multiplication - Place value - Partial products - Compensation - Rounding - Lattice multiplication • How could breaking apart arrays help with multiplying greater numbers? • How could arrays, partial products, or compensation be used to explain the following? 3×10 7×20 2×16 2×125 14×32 4×100 8×50 3×19 4×375 16×54 $6 \times 1,000$ 9×60 5×34 6×625 18×76 • How could equations, arrays, partial products, or compensation be used in the following scenarios? - What is the total number of seats in a high school stadium consisting of 4 sections that contain 100 people? - What is the total number of pennies if Madison has 8 rolls that each contain 100 pennies? - What is the total number of parking spaces in a parking lot that has 8 rows with 30 spaces in each row? • How could equations, arrays, or partial products be used in the following situations? - Susie is buying two chairs that cost $45 each. The tax on each chair is $3. What is the total cost of the chair? - Ms. Perdue's class checks out 25 books from the school library each week over the course of a 9-week quarter. Ms. Martin's class checks out 7 fewer books than Ms. Perdue's class each week. How many books did Ms. Perdue's and Ms. Martin's classes check out over the course of 3 weeks? 6 weeks? 9 weeks? What is the total number of books both classes checked out for the entire quarter?

What Good Hypothetical Questions Do

Good hypothetical questions focus on the possibility and potential of circumstances and conditions—particularly through different scenarios that encourage students to do the following:

• **Imagine** what if.

• **Hypothesize** what would happen, what could happen, how may, or how might.

- **Consider** how could, how would, what else, or how else.
- **Hypothesize** what could be the reason or what would be the reason.
- **Predict** what will or how will.

Hypothetical questions address the cognitive rigor of college- and career-ready standards at the deepest levels cited by Bloom and Webb—specifically, thinking creatively and strategically about *how could* knowledge be used. They also extend students' thinking by providing hypothetical scenarios and situations in which they can use what they have learned.

Unlike other good questions, however, hypothetical questions are not restricted by the details, rules, and specifics governing concepts and procedures—at least, not initially. These are the good questions that encourage students to tap into their imagination and think freely about *what if*—which is the question stem that prompts creative thinking. Then they use the knowledge they have acquired and developed to verify if their ideas, hypotheses, predictions, or theories are valid or viable.

Hypotheses and Predictions

Hypothetical questions generally engage students in two different cognitive processes: predicting and hypothesizing. Although they are often used synonymously, questioning actually engages students in two separate cognitive actions.

A hypothetical question is not, however, a formal hypothesis. A hypothesis is a plausible explanation or possible reason an event or phenomenon occurred, based on evidence, observations, or patterns. A hypothetical question prompts students to form a hypothesis by asking them to speculate or theorize *what if*. Consider how the hypothetical questions in the following scenario prompt students to make educated guesses and tentative statements about chemical reactions.

You are teaching a unit on matter and its interactions. Your students are expected to do the following:

- Construct and revise an explanation for the outcome of a simple chemical reaction based on the outermost electron states of atoms, trends in the periodic table, and knowledge of the patterns of chemical properties. (NGSS-HS-PS1-2)

Your students will address the good questions in Figure 6.2.

Figure 6.2   Good Hypothetical Questions: Matter

HYPOTHETICAL	• What could be the reason for the following reactions? - The flame of a gas grill combusts but the temperature does not rise above 350°F. - A car in a desert shows evidence and signs of rust - M&Ms melt in your mouth but not in your hands • A scale model of a volcano containing hot water, dishwater detergent, and red food coloring erupts when vinegar and baking soda are added. - Water placed in a sealed container kept in a freezer for 2 hours and 45 minutes will flash freeze with a sharp jolt to the bottle. - Soap made from guava leaf extract and sodium hydroxide treats acne. - A light bulb illuminates when connected to a zinc and copper nail inserted into half a slice of citrus (lemon, lime, orange, grapefruit). - A fluffed-up steel wool pad simulates fireworks when lit by a flame.

Notice how these hypothetical questions prompt students to explore the reasons behind an event or outcome (what could have happened or might be the reason). The response to this question will be the hypothesis students use to test and validate their ideas as theories and eventually draw their conclusions. However, students need to acquire further evidence to make their hypotheses logical and ultimately validate them.

A prediction is a forecast driven by evidence or derived from imagination (what could occur). Consider how the following hypothetical questions engage students to make predictions about how patterns and movements of human populations will affect future geographical conditions on Earth.

You are teaching a geography unit on the spatial patterns and movements of human populations. Your students are expected to do the following:

• Explain how cultural and environmental characteristics affect the distribution and movement of people, goods, and ideas; how changes in transportation and communication technology influence the spatial connections among human settlements and affect the diffusion of ideas and cultural practices; analyze the reciprocal nature of how historical events and the spatial diffusion of ideas, technologies, and cultural practices have influenced migration patterns and the distribution of human population. (C3.D2.Geo.7.3-12)

• Analyze and explain how human settlements and movements relate to the locations and use of various natural resources; how relationships between humans and environments extend or contract spatial patterns of settlement and movement; evaluate the impact of economic activities and political decisions on spatial patterns within and among urban, suburban, and rural regions. (C3.D2.Geo.8.3-12)

- Analyze the effects of catastrophic environmental and technological events on human settlements and migration; evaluate the influences of long-term human-induced environmental change on spatial patterns of conflict and cooperation; evaluate the influence of long-term climate variability on human migration and settlement patterns, resource use, and land uses at local-to-global scales. (C3.D2.Geo.9.3-12)

Your students will address the good questions in Figure 6.3.

Figure 6.3   Good Hypothetical Questions: Patterns of Human Populations

HYPOTHETICAL	• How could relationships between humans and environments extend or contract spatial patterns of settlement and movement?
	• How could economic activities and political decisions affect spatial patterns within and among the following regions?
	  - Urban
	  - Suburban
	  - Rural
	• How could catastrophic environmental and technological events affect human settlements and migration?
	• How could long-term human-induced environmental change influence spatial patterns of conflict and cooperation?
	• How could long-term climate variability affect the following at local-to-global scales?
	  - Human migration and settlement patterns
	  - Resources
	  - Land formations

These hypothetical questions also prompt students to draw conclusions and generate ideas about certain events and outcomes. Although these questions can be imaginative as well as evidentiary, it is not possible for students to validate the predictions. That's why it's important to clarify the intent of a hypothetical question and whether the purpose is to make accurate predictions about future outcomes.

Scenarios

Hypothetical questions provide students with different scenarios that prompt them to think critically and creatively about *how could* or *how would* they use what they have learned in an academic or real-world situation. They also engage students to consider what could happen or what would happen given certain patterns, parameters, or provisions. Consider how the following scenario engages students to consider *how could* natural selection and adaptation cause changes in living organisms.

You are teaching a unit on the unity and diversity of biological evolution. Your students are expected to do the following:

- Construct an explanation based on evidence that describes how genetic variations of traits in a population increase some individuals' probability of surviving and reproducing in a specific environment. (NGSS-MS-LS4-4)

- Gather and synthesize information about the technologies that have changed the way humans influence the inheritance of desired traits in organisms. (NGSS-MS-LS4-5)

- Use mathematical representations to support explanations of how natural selection may lead to increases and decreases of specific traits in populations over time. (NGSS-MS-LS4-6)

Your students will address the good questions in Figure 6.4.

Figure 6.4   Good Hypothetical Questions: Evolution

HYPOTHETICAL	• How might genetic variation among organisms affect survival and reproduction?
	• How could genetic variations of traits in a population increase some individuals' chances and probability of surviving and reproducing in a specific environment?

	• How might the differences in characteristics among individuals of the same species provide advantages in the following aspects?
	  - Surviving
	  - Finding mates
	  - Reproducing

	• How may natural selection lead to increases and decreases of specific traits in populations over time?
	• How might natural selection lead to the predominance of certain inherited traits in a population and the suppression of others?
	• What would happen if the trait differences in organisms did not affect reproductive success?
	• How could artificial selection provide humans with the capacity to influence certain characteristics of organisms?
	• How might artificial selection change the way humans influence the inheritance of desired traits in organisms?
	• What could happen if advances in science provided humans with the ability and opportunity to choose the traits in organisms?

The hypothetical questions in Figure 6.4 engage students to contemplate different scenarios and consider myriad outcomes. Students can also create and contribute their own ideas and theories concerning how artificial and natural selection could affect an organism's survival, ability to find a mate, and chances of reproduction. They would use the knowledge they have acquired and developed about artificial and natural selection from their research, examinations, and investigations as evidence to validate their ideas.

Hypothetical questions also provide teachers the opportunity to think creatively about *how could* we come up with and present students different real-world scenarios in which they could use what we're teaching them. For example, in math, we can ask students *how could the mathematical concept and process be used in the following real-world situations* and then pose different scenarios under that question. This would deepen students' relevant knowledge of *how could* the math they are learning be applied in a real-world situation and help them envision or role-play *what would* that experience be like. We can also use hypothetical questions to develop cross-curricular activities for students to share the depth of their learning through creative writing. For example, we can ask students to contemplate *what if* scenarios presented in history/social studies or science class and then have them share their ideas about *what would happen* in a literary narrative text such as a short story, poem, song, or screenplay in their English language arts class.

Metacognitive Knowledge

Hypothetical questions also engage students to consider *what or how else* a correct answer, desired outcome, or specific result can be achieved using different methodologies, models, strategies, and techniques. Anderson and Krathwohl (2001) define this as metacognitive knowledge—knowledge of *how and why could* different concepts and procedures be used to produce the same answer, outcome, or result. With these hypothetical questions, students learn there might be more than one way to answer a question, address a problem, or accomplish a task. They also develop self-knowledge and awareness of different methodologies and strategies they could use that may be more applicable to their learning style. For example, we can ask hypothetical questions to engage students in experimenting with different ways of performing calculations using the four operations of arithmetic and inevitably decide which method would work best for them.

Hypothetical questions also engage students to consider all choices and options before drawing conclusions and making decisions. Consider how the following scenario engages students to consider ways that humans can minimize their influence on Earth.

You are teaching a unit on how humans affect Earth's systems. Your students are expected to do the following:

- Apply scientific principles to design a method for monitoring and minimizing human impact on the environment. (NGSS-MS-ESS3-3)

Your students will address the good questions in Figure 6.5.

Figure 6.5   Good Hypothetical Questions: Human Influence on the Environment

HYPOTHETICAL	• How could the following enhance biodiversity? - Provisioning services that involve the production of renewable resources - Regulating services that increase and decrease environmental change - Sociocultural services that represent human value and enjoyment • How could the following options monitor and minimize human influences on biodiversity in the environment? - Climate regulation - Disease and pest control - Water purification - Biodiversity banking - Gene banking - Reducing use of and improving the targeting of pesticides - Location-specific approaches to protecting migratory species - Establishing wildlife corridors, habitat corridors, and green corridors - Establishing protected areas such as national parks, wildlife sanctuaries, forest reserves, zoological parks, and botanical gardens - Passing and implementing global agreements and national laws • How could the following human influences on biodiversity be minimized and monitored? - Habitat destruction through overconsumption, overpopulation, deforestation, poor land use, air pollution, water pollution, soil contamination, and global warming - Introduction of invasive species due to the breaching of natural barriers and relocation - Genetic pollution through hybridization introgression and genetic swamping - Overexploitation due to excessive hunting and logging, poor soil conservation, and illegal wildlife trade - Decreases in food production, resources, and security due to genetic erosion and genetic pollution - Habitat fragmentation through land conversion and urbanization - Global warming and climate change

The first two questions in Figure 6.5 engage students to examine how different options could enhance biodiversity and minimize changes caused by humans. The last question encourages students to investigate how specific human influences and actions on biodiversity can be minimized and monitored. Each question deepens students' knowledge and thinking and guides them to recognize that there may be more than one method of solving the problem. This freedom to consider a range of possibilities allows students to draw their own conclusions and make their own decisions about how to respond. We will discuss this further in subsequent chapters that discuss argumentative, affective, and personal questions.

Creativity and Curiosity

Hypothetical questions also permit students to use both their education and imagination to imagine *what if*, which is a powerful way to spark students' creativity and curiosity. It releases them "from the world of fact and reality and [allows them to be] free to roam where, perhaps, no one has ever been or ever will be" (Raths, Wasserman, Jonas, & Rothstein, 1986, p. 14). Then they validate whether their ideas are practical or have potential using the academic knowledge and understanding they have acquired and developed.

Consider how a good question engages students to imagine *what if* a natural disaster such as an earthquake or a tsunami struck the West Coast? What could be done to predict, prevent, or protect people from the devastation of such disasters? What kind of technology could be developed and used to make such predictions, prevent such events, or provide protection? Hypothetical questions such as these pique students' curiosity to investigate the potential of such events and to imagine the possibility of designing or inventing something that could handle or harness such events. That's the power of asking students to imagine *what if.* Just as asking *how and why* prompts students to think critically about what they are learning through analysis and evaluation, *what if* encourages students to think creatively through innovation, invention, and design. These good questions will inevitably lead students to demonstrate and develop talent and thinking through creative design.

How Can We Teach Using Good Hypothetical Questions?

To develop good hypothetical questions, use the following formula:

I wonder + Hypothetical Question Stem + DOK Context

Teachers can use this formula to develop those good questions that will pique students' curiosity, imagination, interest, and wonder and prompt them to think critically and creatively about what they are learning. Let's take a look at how good hypothetical questions foster critical and creative thinking.

English Language Arts, Fine Arts, Visual Arts

Good hypothetical questions incite both critical and creative thinking in literature, art, and music. Think about the main idea, plot, or theme of any literary text and then turn it into a question that begins with the appropriate good hypothetical question stem.

Hypothetical questions engage students to think critically about broader ideas associated with a specific text or author and can be used to pique students' curiosity and interest in reading texts of literary fiction and nonfiction. That's how these works were created—as a response to a good hypothetical question that asked the author or artist to imagine *what if*, consider *what could or what would happen*, or predict *what will*.

Hypothetical questions prompt students to think critically about central ideas and themes expressed in a specific text or by an author. Consider how the following scenario engages students to think critically about the ideas expressed in a text.

You are teaching a book study on *Fahrenheit 451* by Ray Bradbury. Your students are expected to do the following:

- Determine central ideas or themes of a text and analyze their development; summarize the key supporting details and ideas. (CCSS.ELA-LITERACY.CCRA.R.2)

- Analyze how and why individuals, events, or ideas develop and interact over the course of a text. (CCSS.ELA-LITERACY.CCRA.R.3)

- Assess how point of view or purpose shapes the content and style of a text. (CCSS.ELA-LITERACY.CCRA.R.6)

- Integrate and evaluate content presented in diverse media and formats, including visually and quantitatively, as well as in words. (CCSS.ELA-LITERACY.CCRA.R.7)

- Write informative/explanatory texts to examine and convey complex ideas and information clearly and accurately through the effective selection, organization, and analysis of content. (CCSS.ELA-LITERACY.CCRA.W.2)

- Draw evidence from literary or informational texts to support analysis, reflection, and research. (CCSS.ELA-LITERACY.CCRA.W.9)

Your students will address the good questions in Figure 6.6.

Consider what *Fahrenheit 451* and other science fiction texts address—*what will life be like in the future* and *how could the past and the present affect and influence the future*. Those are very broad and grand ideas and topics for students to consider, which makes them good universal questions that spark students' curiosity. They also encourage students to think critically about *what if people were forbidden to read, what if the world were like the one portrayed in Bradbury's science fiction novel,* and *what is the potential for our future?*

Figure 6.6   Good Hypothetical Questions: Ray Bradbury's *Fahrenheit 451*

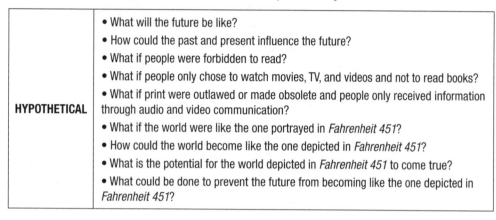

HYPOTHETICAL	• What will the future be like? • How could the past and present influence the future? • What if people were forbidden to read? • What if people only chose to watch movies, TV, and videos and not to read books? • What if print were outlawed or made obsolete and people only received information through audio and video communication? • What if the world were like the one portrayed in *Fahrenheit 451*? • How could the world become like the one depicted in *Fahrenheit 451*? • What is the potential for the world depicted in *Fahrenheit 451* to come true? • What could be done to prevent the future from becoming like the one depicted in *Fahrenheit 451*?

When it comes to fostering and promoting cognitive rigor in the literary, fine, and visual arts, hypothetical questions will be those inquiries that engage students to understand and to engage in the cognitive process of examining and expressing ideas critically and creatively.

Mathematics

Math hypothetical questions prompt students to respond to three kinds of inquiries. The first asks students to contemplate *how could* mathematical concepts and procedures be used to solve both academic and real-world problems. For example, we can ask students to consider *how could multiplication be used to solve the following math problems* and provide students with problems to solve and explain. The instructional focus becomes can the mathematical concept or operation be used to solve problems, rather than how to solve specific problems. Figure 6.1 (p. 88) includes examples of hypothetical questions that focus on thinking strategically (DOK-3) and explaining *how could* the mathematical concept or procedure be used to solve math problems.

The second kind of mathematical hypothetical question engages students to extend their thinking about *how could* mathematical practices, principles, and processes solve hypothetical real-world problems and situations. The hypothetical scenarios serve as both the context in which students can apply the mathematical concepts and procedures and the textual evidence that students can use to support their responses. For example, suppose you are teaching a lesson on how to apply and extend previous understandings of numbers to the system of rational numbers. Ask students the following question:

> How could positive and negative numbers be used together in the following real-world contexts?
>
> • Measuring temperature above and below sea level
> • Measuring elevation above and below sea level
> • Calculating credits and debits
> • Gauging positive and negative charges

Each context serves as a prompt into an investigation of how the mathematical theorem can be transferred and used to address a hypothetical real-world situation. The emphasis is on extending thinking (DOK-4) rather than solving the problems themselves.

The third kind of hypothetical question asks students to consider *how could* different methods and strategies be used to perform mathematical operations, which extends students' procedural understanding of mathematical processes. See Figure 6.1, p. 88, which asks students to consider *how could* multidigit numbers be multiplied using the methods offered. The instructional focus and assessment is not on solving the problems correctly but on thinking strategically (DOK-3) and extending thinking (DOK-4) about *how and why* these traditional and nontraditional methods can be used. These are the good questions that can be used to address "new math" or "Common Core math" problems. Instead of requiring students to use these routine and nonroutine procedures to solve math problems, we can use hypothetical questions to make learning experiences in math more experimental and investigative.

Science

Teaching and learning for cognitive rigor in science is driven by hypothetical questions. For examples of these questions, see Figures 6.2 through 6.6. These good questions engage students to frame hypotheses and make predictions about natural phenomena by conducting experiments to prove or disprove theories. The responses to hypothetical questions in science can serve as a precursor for a student to design a model or plan that addresses an engineering design issue. Figure 6.7 includes examples of good hypothetical questions that engage students in both scientific inquiry and engineering design. Note how easily these questions could be developed into good driving questions that foster deep education experiences, including project-based and problem-based learning.

Figure 6.7   Good Hypothetical Questions: Engineering Standards

SCIENCE COLLEGE- AND CAREER-READY STANDARDS	GOOD HYPOTHETICAL QUESTIONS (ENGINEERING DESIGN)
Use tools and materials to design and build a structure that will reduce the warming effect of sunlight on an area. (NGSS-K-PS3-2)	• How could the warming effect of sunlight on an area be reduced? • What could be designed and built to reduce the warming effect of sunlight on an area?
Use tools and materials to design and build a device that uses light or sound to solve the problem of communicating over distance. (NGSS-1-PS4-4)	• How could light and sound be used to communicate over a distance? • What could be designed that uses light or sound to solve the problem of communicating over a distance?
Compare multiple solutions designed to slow or prevent wind or water from changing the shape of the land. (NGSS-2-ESS2-1)	• How could wind or water be slowed or prevented from changing the shape of the land? • What could be done to slow or prevent wind or water from changing the shape of land?
Make a claim about the merit of a design solution that reduces the impacts of a weather-related hazard. (NGSS-3-ESS3-1)	• What could be done to reduce the effects of a weather-related hazard? • How could different solutions reduce the effects of weather hazards effectively?
Generate and compare multiple solutions to reduce the impacts of natural Earth processes on humans. (NGSS-4-ESS3-2)	• What could be done to reduce the effects of natural Earth processes on humans?
Obtain and combine information about ways individual communities use science ideas to protect the Earth's resources and environment. (NGSS-5-ESS3-1)	• How could individual communities use science ideas to protect Earth's resources and environment?
Apply scientific principles to design, construct, and test a device that either minimizes or maximizes thermal energy transfer. (NGSS-MS-PS3-3)	• How could thermal energy transfer be minimized or maximized? • What could be designed or constructed that would minimize or maximize thermal energy transfer? • How could scientific principles be applied to design, construct, and test a device that minimizes or maximizes energy transfer?

(continued)

Figure 6.7   Good Hypothetical Questions: Engineering Standards (*continued*)

SCIENCE COLLEGE- AND CAREER-READY STANDARDS	GOOD HYPOTHETICAL QUESTIONS (ENGINEERING DESIGN)
Evaluate competing design solutions for maintaining biodiversity and ecosystem services. (NGSS-MS-LS2-5)	• How could biodiversity and ecosystem services be maintained? • How could different design solutions maintain biodiversity and ecosystem services effectively?
Apply scientific principles to design a method for monitoring and minimizing a human impact on the environment. (NGSS-MS-ESS3-4)	• How could human influence on the environment be monitored and minimized? • What kind of method could be designed to monitor and minimize human influences on the environment? • How could scientific principles be used to design a method for monitoring and minimizing human influences on the environment?
Design, build, and refine a device that works within given constraints to convert one form of energy into another form of energy. (NGSS-HS-PS3-3)	• How could energy be converted from one form to another? • What kind of device could be designed, built, and refined that works within given constraints to convert one form of energy into another?
Design, evaluate, and refine a solution for reducing the impacts of human activities on the environment and biodiversity. (NGSS-HS-LS2-7)	• What could be done to reduce the effects of human activities on the environment and biodiversity?
Evaluate competing design solutions for developing, managing, and utilizing energy and mineral resources based on cost-benefit ratios. (NGSS-HS-ESS3-2)	• What could be developed to manage and use energy and mineral resources based on cost-benefit ratios?

History and Social Studies

Use good hypothetical questions to engage students in history and social studies by asking them to frame hypotheses and make predictions based upon historical data or information. These questions deepen students' awareness of historical ideas, incidents, individuals, and issues by fostering counterfactual thinking—or creating alternative versions of events. Counterfactual thinking in history is a subgenre of study that Black and MacRaild (2007) call "what if" history—"the idea of conjecturing on what did not happen, or what might have happened, in order to understand what did happen" (p. 125).

- What if early human civilization began and flourished in the Americas instead of the Near East?
- What if explorers from China or Japan discovered North and South America prior to the Western Europeans?
- What if Alexander the Great did not die at such a young age?
- What if the Roman Empire never fell or was able to regain power during the Middle Ages?
- What if the Egyptian civilization never collapsed?
- What if the Renaissance never happened?
- What if the Spartans were able to hold off the Persians at the Battle of Thermopylae?
- What if Christopher Columbus never reached the New World?
- What if the Byzantines were never defeated and the Ottoman Turks never rose to power after the Byzantine-Ottoman War?
- What if the colonists lost the American Revolution?

These good questions provide students the opportunity to think critically and creatively about history and the effects of consequential and inconsequential events and experiences.

Conclusion

Of all the cognitive rigor questions in the framework, good hypothetical questions are the most dynamic because they engage students to think critically and creatively about what they are learning. They challenge students to think strategically about *what else* and *how else* they can attain and explain answers, outcomes, and results. They also extend students' thinking by engaging them to consider *how could* and *how would* they transfer and use what they have learned in different academic and real-world contexts. Most important, hypothetical questions test the boundaries of the knowledge and imagination of both students and teachers by encouraging us to imagine *what if*, hypothesize *what could* or *would happen*, or predict *what will* and verifying whether our thinking is valid and viable.

PROFESSIONAL DEVELOPMENT

How to Develop Good Hypothetical Questions to Pique Curiosity and Creativity

Objective

Develop good hypothetical questions that challenge students to think critically and creatively about *what if, what could happen, what would happen,* and *what would happen* and think flexibly about *how could* they transfer and use the deeper knowledge they have acquired.

Materials

- College- and career-ready standards adopted by your state
- Curriculum and texts adopted by your school
- Good Questions and Bloom's Taxonomy (Figure 1.2)
- Good Questions and Depth of Knowledge (Figure 1.4)

Procedure

1. Identify the academic standards, texts, and topics that will be addressed as part of the lesson or unit.

2. Define *what are the specific details and elements* that will be addressed as part of the lesson or unit.

3. Describe *what are the concepts and procedures* that will be examined and investigated as part of the lesson or unit.

4. Determine what kind of thinking students are to demonstrate, and place the statement defining the detail, element, concept, or procedure next to the appropriate question stem in Figure 6.8.

a. If the student is expected to imagine, then place the statement next to the question stem *what if.*

b. If the student is expected to consider, then place the statement next to the question stem *how could, how would, what else,* or *how else.*

c. If the student is expected to hypothesize, then place the statement next to the question stem *what could happen, what would happen, how may,* or *how might.* (For mathematical investigations or scientific experiments, place the hypothetical scenarios and situations under the question stem.)

d. If the student is expected to predict, then place the statement next to the question stem *what will* or *how will.*

Figure 6.8   Good Hypothetical Questions Generator

IMAGINE	I wonder	What if	
CONSIDER	I wonder	How could	
		How would	
		What else	
		How else	
HYPOTHESIZE	I wonder	What could happen	
		What would happen	
		How may	
		How might	
PREDICT	I wonder	What will	
		How will	

7

How Do Good Argumentative Questions Address Choices, Claims, and Controversies?

You are teaching a lesson on Earth and the solar system. Your students are expected to do the following:

- Analyze and interpret data to determine scale properties of objects in the solar system. (NGSS-MS-ESS1-3)

Your students will respond to the good questions in Figure 7.1.

Answers to assessment questions are either correct or incorrect, but cognitive rigor questions demand that both an assessment and instruction be more nuanced; that is, they require students to elaborate and explain how and why their answers are accurate, acceptable, and even appropriate. Factual questions expect students to provide details. Analytical and reflective questions challenge students to go in depth. Hypothetical questions engage students to deliberate *what if* and determine possibilities and potential. As we move down the framework, responses to good questions are not assessed as correct or incorrect but rather evaluated as right or wrong based upon how the response is crafted and the specific elements of the evidence presented. For example, what is the right answer to these good argumentative questions?

• Is it accurate to declare that Pluto is not a planet based upon the evidence provided by the International Astronomical Union (IAU) General Assembly (2006)?

• Is it accurate to assert Pluto should be categorized as a planet based upon reasoning provided by the Harvard-Smithsonian Center for Astrophysics (2014), whose participants voted to classify Pluto as a planet?

• Is it appropriate to suggest that Pluto's planetary status seems to be a matter of semantics as well as science?

Figure 7.1

ARGUMENTATIVE	• Should Pluto be reclassified as a planet or continue to be designated as a dwarf planet? • Is the IAU's definition of a planet based upon scientific fact or expert opinion? • Whose definition of a planet should be considered authoritative and final—the IAU's or the Harvard-Smithsonian Center for Astrophysics'?

A variety of responses could be considered accurate and acceptable. The strength of the answers, and whether they are *right or wrong*, depends upon how clearly, comprehensively, and convincingly they are framed. It is also appropriate to disagree or refute the response and even provide a rebuttal that presents the other side of the issue or argument. That's the next aspect of teaching and learning for cognitive rigor—to have students use the evidence they gather and expertise they develop to draw conclusions and defend decisions.

What Good Argumentative Questions Do

Good argumentative questions engage students to explore all sides of an issue or topic and make a choice or take a position that is logical and defendable. To give these sorts of answers, students must do the following:

• **Consider** multiple perspectives, points of view (including their own), and positions on a text or topic.

• **Critique** the accuracy and validity of conclusions and contentions.

• **Craft** arguments supported by valid reasoning and relevant and sufficient evidence.

Argumentative questions are not meant to be combative, opinionated, or persuasive—though they can be. The goal of these good questions is *not* for students to learn how to win an argument but rather how "to present their own argument or take someone else's apart" (Rose, 1989) and "to transform students into not just better arguers, but also more critical thinkers who are adept at constructing evidence-based arguments" (Britannica Digital Learning, 2014, p. 2).

Argumentative questions ask students to keep an open mind and do relevant research to make solid arguments and sound decisions. They teach students not to make choices and decisions based upon personal emotions or experience alone. Most important, these questions help students recognize that there are three ways a good question that promotes cognitive rigor can be answered: correctly, incorrectly, or convincingly as a claim or conclusion. Note, however, that claims and conclusions are conditional and can change if further information is presented or a fresh perspective is provided.

Argumentative questions, as well as other good questions rooted in cognitive rigor, prompt students to comment on and critique ideas and issues based upon the evidence. Students are challenged to analyze the data and details as they are presented and determine if they are valid and unbiased. They are encouraged to assess their own thinking and to offer and decide whether their perspective is based primarily upon facts or feelings. Let's take a closer look at how good argumentative questions engage students to evaluate specific claims that are strengthened with valid reasoning and sufficient evidence.

Choices

Argumentative questions are truly multiple-choice questions, but they are unlike typical multiple-choice questions that ask students to recognize and select the correct answer from the three distractors. Argumentative questions "require a decision that needs to be selected from a number of competing alternatives" (Jonassen & Hung, 2008, p. 17). Argumentative questions ask students to consider options that are all valid, defensible choices. The objective is for students to evaluate the strengths and weaknesses of the different options, make an informed decision about which one is right, and defend their choice with logical reasoning and credible evidence.

The phrasing of argumentative questions does pose a validity and usefulness risk because an incorrectly phrased question could be responded to with a simple *yes* or *no*. Other incorrectly phrased questions may inadvertently direct students to a particular position. To avoid this, rephrase the question as an *either/or* inquiry and ask which one is the best, most appropriate, or most effective.

For example, we should not pose questions such as *should animal testing be banned?* Students can simply answer *yes* or *no* and end the discussion. We should rephrase the question to ask *should animal testing be banned, permitted, regulated, or reserved for special situations?* Now you're asking students to explore all sides of the issue, make a choice, and defend their conclusion. Phrasing questions like this teaches students that some questions cannot be answered with a clear-cut *yes* or *no* but require a response of *it depends* and an explanation of *how* or *why*.

Claims

Argumentative questions engage students to evaluate the following types of arguments and specific claims:

- Claims of **facts**—Is the claim based upon fact, opinion, or inference?
- Claims of **definition**—Is the claim definitive, conditional, or interpretive?
- Claims of **cause**—Is the claim about a reason or result valid, invalid, or questionable?
- Claims of **value**—Is the claim about the importance or worth of something accurate, acceptable, or appropriate based upon a scale of values or set of standards?
- Claims of **policy**—How should an issue or problem be addressed? (Wood, 2007)

Claims are not facts. A fact is an objective statement that has been verified. Claims are positions that can be defended as being *right*. For example, it's a fact that Pluto is a celestial body in the solar system as proven through valid data obtained through scientific research. Whether Pluto is a planet depends upon the interpretation of what defines or qualifies as a planet.

According to the IAU's definition, Pluto is not a planet. However, the Harvard-Smithsonian Center for Astrophysics claims Pluto is a planet. Each group has reasons and evidence that support their interpretation of Pluto's status. That's why the designation of Pluto's planetary status is not a claim of fact but a position that needs to be defended. The claim of an argumentative question serves a dual purpose.

The argumentative question addresses the assertion, declaration, or statement that is to be debated and discussed. Different argumentative questions are offered in Figure 7.2. Each question addresses a specific claim that must be proven as factual, definitive, appropriate, or viable to be considered *right*. The strength of these claims—both the ones in the questions asked and the responses given—are gauged based upon the following criteria:

- Evidence and proof—Is it accurate? Is it credible? Is it factual? Is it relevant? Is it sufficient? Is it true?

• Logic and reasoning—Is it plausible? Is it possible? Is it rational? Is it sensible? Is it valid?

• Value and worth—Is it acceptable? Is it appropriate? Is it feasible? Is it practical? Is it sensible? Is it viable?

Figure 7.2   Five Types of Argumentative Questions

ARGUMENTATIVE	Fact	• Can stem cell research provide deeper insight into the basics of the human body and potentially help treat medical issues, or is its scientific value unproven, overstated, or flawed? • Does adding time to the school day or year increase, decrease, or have no effect on student learning? • Is technology increasing, decreasing, or changing the way people think and learn? • Are women more or less effective than men in combat? • Has industrialization produced more benefits or problems for society? • Is Bigfoot real, a myth, or another type of creature that has been misidentified?
	Definition	• Is obesity a physical condition, a mental illness, or a social issue? • Is global warming a natural phenomenon or a human-created event? • What is true beauty? • What are the legal, religious, and social definitions of marriage? • What defines a work as art or pornography? • Is a fetus a human being or a group of cells? • What is a justified war versus an unjustified war? • What is considered to be sexual harassment?
	Cause	• Are the increases in severe weather patterns a result of global warming, or are they a natural cycle of Earth's systems? • Does overeating lead to disease and death? • Is the AIDS epidemic due to inadequate funding for research or human behavior? • Is putting infants in daycare beneficial or detrimental to a child's development? • Which has a bigger influence on the quality of an education a child receives— poverty or stability?
	Value	• Should vaccinations for children be mandatory or optional? • Should the United States involve itself in global conflicts, or should the nation be more concerned with domestic affairs? • Should children be recognized and rewarded for participation, performance, or both? • Are public schools better or worse than private schools? • Is torture a justifiable or unjustifiable means of punishment? • What makes a better pet: cats, dogs, fish, or a more exotic animal? • Is euthanasia moral or immoral? • Are cell phones tools for instruction or weapons of mass distraction?

ARGUMENTATIVE	**Policy**	• What role should the United States play in global conflicts? • Should the states adopt national academic standards or develop their own academic standards? • Should the minimum wage be raised, lowered, or reflect the cost of living in a particular location? • How should the use of cell phones during driving be handled? • Should felons keep or lose their right to vote? • Should public smoking be banned, permitted, or regulated? • Should U.S. presidents be allowed to continue to serve up to two terms, should they be allowed to serve more than two terms, or should they be allowed to run again after a specific period of time has elapsed?

Even if a claim is defended as *right*, a position could change if new information is discovered. Again, look at the argument about Pluto. Although most experts and professional organizations have accepted the IAU's definition of a planet as *right*, further details and new information may change this definition.

Controversies

Argumentative questions also engage students to tackle controversies and encourage critical and creative thinking. Graff (2003) calls this instructional approach "teaching the conflicts" and "learning by controversy"—delineating what the conflicting claims are and how they should be addressed. Here are some ways to encourage critical and creative inquiry:

- What is the controversy?
- What should be done about the controversy?
- How should the controversy be addressed?
- Why should the controversy be addressed?
- What is needed or necessary to address and respond to the controversy?
- Should the controversy be addressed, handled, resolved, settled—or avoided?

The goal of controversial argumentative questions is not to solve the problem. There are too many stakeholders with subjective points of view for that to happen. Some people may claim there is a serious issue that *should* be addressed. Others may present a counterclaim that refutes this position. That's why asking *what is the controversy* is argumentative. It depends on a person's point of view and how they perceive the conflict.

So why attempt to respond to controversial argumentative questions if they are so difficult to address? Because these are the real-world problems "that plague our cities and our world and touch each and every one of us" (Kolko, 2012). Each critical controversy addresses a cultural, environmental, political, or socioeconomic issue or situation that has multiple causes and serious consequences. Rittel and Webber (1973) call these critical controversies *wicked problems*; that is, ill-structured problems that are complicated to define due to factors including the accuracy and amount of information available; the legal, political, and socioeconomic consequences and liabilities; the number of stakeholders; and related problems that could arise (Kolko, 2012). The constraints in responding to these critical controversies make any attempts to do so "impossible projects" (Dobson, 2013).

The inherent difficulty in addressing these issues does not mean educators should avoid them. In fact, it is this difficulty that argues strongly for addressing these issues as part of the educational experience. See Appendix D for a list of good argumentative questions that challenge students to determine and discuss whether a wicked problem or impossible project should be addressed, handled, settled, resolved—or avoided.

How Can We Teach with Good Argumentative Questions?

Traditionally, argumentative questions have been used to teach students how to influence others through debate and persuasion. Although debate and persuasion are ways to address good argumentative questions, they are not the primary goal. When students address argumentative questions, they are prompted to discuss the following:

- Is the claim accurate, inaccurate, or questionable?
- Is the conclusion definitive, inconclusive, or tentative?
- Is the contention irrefutable, disputable, or unresolvable?

These are the guiding questions that foster argumentative literacy or the ability to listen, summarize, and respond to ideas, information, and issues (Graff, 2003). These cognitive skills are what Graff (2003) claims to be "rightly viewed as central to being educated" and measure college and career readiness (p. 3). In fact, the performance objectives of college- and career-ready standards in all subject areas place emphasis on expressing knowledge and thinking through argumentation (NCCAS, 2015; NCSS, 2013; NGACBP & CCSSO, 2010; NGSS Lead States, 2013). Let's take a look at how argumentative questions foster decision making and discussion about texts and topics across various curriculums.

English Language Arts, Fine Arts, Visual Arts

Argumentation is a core college- and career-ready idea that is heavily emphasized in the English language arts academic standards. Each domain includes performance objectives that challenge students to address the following overarching essential questions:

- How can the argument and specific claims in a text, including the validity of the reasoning and the relevance and sufficiency of the evidence, be delineated and evaluated?

- How can arguments be written to support claims in an analysis of substantive topics or texts using valid reasoning and relevant, sufficient evidence?

- How can information, findings, and supporting evidence be presented in a style appropriate to the task, purpose, and audience so that listeners can follow the line of reasoning, organization, development, and style?

The overarching essential questions are more analytical than argumentative because they ask students to communicate how to explain or evaluate arguments. The central idea of a specific argumentative question can come from anywhere—not necessarily from the curriculum. Use these questions to teach argumentation as a competency that students can develop.

Good argumentative questions engage students to defend specific literary texts, artistic, or musical works and require them to validate their reasoning. Consider how the following good questions prompt students to critique different authors' perspectives on civil disobedience as well as their own thinking on the topic.

Your students are reading and reviewing different texts that address the philosophy and practice of civil disobedience. Your students are expected to do the following:

- Determine central ideas or themes of a text and analyze their development; summarize the key supporting details and ideas. (CCSS.ELA-LITERACY.CCRA.R.2)

- Assess how point of view or purpose shapes the content and style of a text. (CCSS.ELA-LITERACY.CCRA.R.6)

- Delineate and evaluate the argument and specific claims in a text, including the validity of the reasoning as well as the relevance and sufficiency of the evidence. (CCSS.ELA-LITERACY.CCRA.R.8)

- Analyze how two or more texts address similar themes or topics in order to build knowledge or to compare the approaches the authors take. (CCSS.ELA-LITERACY. CCRA.R.9)

- Write arguments to support claims in an analysis of substantive topics or texts using valid reasoning and relevant and sufficient evidence. (CCSS.ELA-LITERACY. CCRA.W.1)

- Draw evidence from literary or informational texts to support analysis, reflection, and research. (CCSS.ELA-LITERACY.CCRA.W.9)

- Evaluate a speaker's point of view, reasoning, and use of evidence and rhetoric. (CCSS.ELA-LITERACY.CCRA.SL.3)

Your students will address and respond to the good questions in Figure 7.3.

Figure 7.3   Good Argumentative Questions: Civil Disobedience

ARGUMENTATIVE	• Whose views on civil disobedience are most or least compatible with a democratic government?
	  - Socrates
	  - St. Thomas Aquinas
	  - John Locke
	  - Henry David Thoreau
	  - Mahatma Gandhi
	  - Dr. Martin Luther King Jr.
	  - John Rawls
	• Is civil disobedience justifiable or unjustifiable in a democratic society?
	• Is it ever permissible or completely unacceptable to break a law?
	• Is demonstrating or protesting through civil disobedience effective or ineffective?
	• Is violence ever justifiable or always unacceptable as an act of civil disobedience?
	• Is civil disobedience appropriate or inappropriate?

Notice how these good questions extend students' thinking from analyzing the central ideas of different texts to defending a claim of value about which one is most or least compatible with the principles of a democratic government. Students are also prompted to draw upon the ideas and information presented in these texts and their own system of values to craft their claim.

The classroom results of this freedom are potentially profound. For example, what if students were encouraged to discuss and defend claims and contentions such as the following:

- Is "The Raven" Edgar Allan Poe's best poem—or is it just his most successful?
- Is *Romeo and Juliet* the best example of a Shakespearean tragedy, or are his other works better examples?
- Is Leonardo da Vinci's *Mona Lisa* celebrated more as a masterpiece of art or for its mystery and mystique?
- Which one of Beethoven's symphonies absolutely reflects the composer's artistry and talent?

These questions and the discussions that follow encourage students to think deeply about the quality of what they are studying as they expand their knowledge about works of art, literature, and music.

Mathematics

Good argumentative questions in math challenge students to use reasoning and proof to construct viable arguments and to critique the reasoning of others (CCSS.MATH.PRACTICE.MP3).

A mathematical proof is an argument or claim that attempts to convince other people that something is true (Hutchings, n.d.). The proof—or claim—can be verified using a verbal statement, an algorithmic formula, a numerical problem, or word problem. Students are challenged to prove that the mathematical claim is absolute (always true), conditional (sometimes true), or faulty (needs more information). Consider how the following argumentative questions engage students to prove whether mathematical statements about performing multiplication and division with decimals are absolute or conditional.

You are teaching a unit on performing operations with multidigit whole numbers and with decimals to hundredths. Your students are expected to do the following:

- Recognize that in a multi-digit number, a digit in one place represents 10 times as much as it represents in the place to its right and 1/10 of what it represents in the place to its left. (CCSS.MATH.CONTENT.5.NBT.A.1)

- Explain patterns in the number of zeros of the product when multiplying a number by powers of 10, and explain patterns in the placement of the decimal point when a decimal is multiplied or divided by a power of 10. Use whole-number exponents to denote powers of 10. (CCSS.MATH.CONTENT.5.NBT.A.2)

- Add, subtract, multiply, and divide decimals to hundredths, using concrete models or drawings and strategies based on place value, properties of operations, and/or the relationship between addition and subtraction; relate the strategy to a written method and explain the reasoning used. (CCSS.MATH.CONTENT.5.NBT.B.7)

Your students will address the good questions in Figure 7.4.

Figure 7.4   Good Argumentative Questions: Multidigit Whole Numbers and Decimals

ARGUMENTATIVE	• What is the proof of the following? - Patterns can be used to mentally multiply and divide decimals by 10, 100, or 1,000. - The product of a whole number or decimal can be estimated by using rounding or compatible numbers. - The standard multiplication algorithm involving decimals is an extension of the standard algorithm for multiplying whole numbers. - The decimal point can be determined by place value or sometimes decided by reasoning about the relative size of numbers. - The product of two decimals less than one is less than either factor. - Estimating quotients for whole-number divisors and dividends can be applied to calculations with decimal dividends and divisors. Some compatible numbers can be used in most cases. - The standard division algorithm involving decimals is an extension of the standard algorithm for dividing whole numbers. - A number divided by a decimal can be represented as an equivalent calculation using place value to change the divisor to a whole number.

These enduring understandings about decimals have been proven true, which makes them math facts. The instructional focus is to determine whether these mathematical statements are true in all circumstances and situations (*absolute*), require further explanation (*faulty*), or depend upon the parameters of the problem (*conditional*).

For example, the claim that the *product of two decimal numbers that are less than one will always be less than either factor* is absolute (always true). The claim that the *decimal point of a number can be determined either by place value or sometimes decided by reasoning about the relative size of numbers* is conditional (sometimes true). Note that both of these claims could be argued to be faulty because they require further elaboration or more information.

Argumentative good questions used in mathematics engage students to express the logic and reasoning behind solutions. Teaching for cognitive rigor requires that students solve the math problem and express the reasoning behind the mathematical concepts to verify their answers. To do that, students break these problems into individual components or steps and defend why these various steps can be taken based upon what they know about mathematical facts and procedures.

Science

Argumentative questions in science engage students in using evidentiary reasoning to defend claims made about scientific events and phenomena. The objective of these questions is for students to prove or disprove a scientific hypothesis or idea. Their arguments "can be based on deductions from premises, on inductive generalizations of existing patterns, or on inferences about the best possible explanation" (NGSS, 2013, p. 71). Consider how the following argumentative questions prompt students to prove the cause-and-effect relationships among common ancestry, biodiversity, natural selection, and adaptation.

You are teaching a unit on the unity and diversity of biological evolution. Your students are expected to do the following:

- Communicate scientific information that common ancestry and biological evolution are supported by multiple lines of empirical evidence. (NGSS-HS-LS4-1)

- Construct an explanation based on evidence that the process of evolution primarily results from four factors: (1) the potential for a species to increase in number; (2) the heritable genetic variation of individuals in a species due to mutation and sexual reproduction; (3) competition for limited resources; and (4) the proliferation of those organisms that are better able to survive and reproduce in the environment. (NGSS-HS-LS4-2)

- Apply concepts of statistics and probability to support explanations that organisms with an advantageous heritable trait tend to increase in proportion to organisms lacking this trait. (NGSS-HS-LS4-3)

- Construct an explanation based on evidence for how natural selection leads to adaptation of populations. (NGSS-HS-LS4-4)

- Evaluate the evidence supporting claims that changes in environmental conditions may result in: (1) increases in the number of individuals of some species; (2) the emergence of new species over time; and (3) the extinction of other species. (NGSS-HS-LS4-5)

Your students will respond to the good questions in Figure 7.5.

Notice the expectations of these standards. They do not challenge students to understand these scientific concepts or explain these natural processes. Each performance objective asks students to construct and support explanations or claims based upon evidence about how heredity and the environment influence the biological evolution of living organisms. They challenge students to gather the evidence that supports these scientific claims and conclusions. They also engage students to respond with their own claims that explain, justify, or support the validity of scientific explanations.

Figure 7.5   Good Argumentative Questions: Evolution

ARGUMENTATIVE	• What is the evidence that different species may be related through common ancestry and biological evolution? • What is the validity of the evidence that evolution could be the result of the following factors? - The potential for a species to increase in number - The heritable genetic variation of individuals in a species due to mutation and sexual reproduction - Competition for resources - The proliferation of organisms that are better able to survive and reproduce in the environment • What is the proof that organisms with an advantageous heritable trait tend to increase in proportion to organisms lacking this trait? • What is the evidence that natural selection leads to adaptation of populations? • What is the evidence that changes in environmental conditions may result in the following? - Increase in the number of individuals of some species - Emergence of new species over time - Extinction of other species

Argumentative questions in science can also be used to engage students to make choices and defend decisions about which design solution is the most effective—or right—to address a real-world problem in science. Consider how the following scenario engages students to evaluate competing design solutions related to ecosystems.

You are teaching a unit on Earth and human activity. Your students are expected to do the following:

• Evaluate competing design solutions for developing, managing, and utilizing energy and mineral resources based on cost-benefit ratios. (NGSS-HS-ESS3-2)

Your students will address and respond to the good questions in Figure 7.6.

Figure 7.6   Good Argumentative Questions: Engineering

ARGUMENTATIVE	• Which design solutions for developing, managing, and using energy and mineral resources would be the most effective based upon cost-benefit ratios?
	
	• Which best practices and design solutions would be most cost-effective to address the following?
	   - Conserving, recycling, and reuse of resources (e.g., minerals, metals)
	   - Farming
	   - Mining coal, tar sands, and oil shades
	   - Pumping petroleum and natural gas

These good questions engage students in problem solving through decision making. The goal is for students to decide which design solutions would provide the best cost-benefit ratios based upon their examinations, experiments, and investigations.

History and Social Studies

Argumentative questions challenge students to question history based on the accuracy and appropriateness of historical, political, and socioeconomic actions, decisions, and events. These good questions challenge students to defend whether a claim is based on fact or interpretation. The questions also draw students into deeper discussions about whether history is presented objectively or based on a perspective of the past. Consider how the following argumentative question engages students to discuss who should truly be acknowledged as the first president of the United States.

You are teaching a unit on the American Revolution related to politics, economy, and society. Your students are expected to do the following:

• Understand revolutionary government-making at the national and state levels. (NHS. USE3.2)

• Generate and use questions about individuals and groups who have shaped significant historical changes and continuities; analyze why they and the developments they shaped are seen as historically significant; and assess how the significance of their actions changes over time and is shaped by the historical context. (C3. D2.His.3.3-12)

- Describe and analyze how people's perspectives shaped the historical sources they created, how people's perspectives influenced what information is available in the historical sources they created, and the ways in which the perspectives of those writing history shaped the history that they produced. (C3.D2.His.6.3-12)

Your students will address and respond to the good argumentative questions in Figure 7.7.

Figure 7.7   Good Argumentative Questions: George Washington

ARGUMENTATIVE	• Should George Washington continue to be acknowledged as the first president of the United States, or should the eight presidents appointed under the Articles of Confederation be acknowledged?

It is true that George Washington was the first president of the United States who was elected under the U.S. Constitution. It's also a fact that eight U.S. men served a one-year term as "Presidents of the United States Under Congress Assembled" under the Articles of Confederation prior to Washington's election. The argument is not about whether Washington should be known as the first president elected under the U.S. Constitution but whether these other eight men should be acknowledged as U.S. presidents. The objective is for students to explore both sides of the issue and make their choice and defend it clearly, comprehensively, and convincingly.

Argumentative questions in history also provide students the opportunity to express whether a historical decision was justified. These good questions engage students to conduct case studies about historical actions, events, and issues in which they critique how the situation was addressed. Consider how the following argumentative questions provide students the opportunity to comment on the actions and decisions made by the United States during World War II.

You are teaching a unit on the causes and course of World War II, the character of the war at home and abroad, and how the war reshaped the U.S. role in world affairs. Your students are expected to do the following:

- Evaluate American responses to German, Italian, and Japanese aggression in Europe, Africa, and Asia from 1935 to 1941. (NHS.USE8.3.A.5)

- Evaluate the decision to employ nuclear weapons against Japan and assess later controversies over the decision. (NHS.USE8.3.B.4)

- Evaluate the internment of Japanese Americans during the war and assess the implication for civil liberties. (NHS.USE8.3.C.4)

Your students will address and respond to the good questions in Figure 7.8.

Figure 7.8   Good Argumentative Questions: World War II

ARGUMENTATIVE	• Was the United States right or wrong to maintain an isolationist position in World War II?
	 • Was Japan's decision to bomb Pearl Harbor wise, foolish, or reckless?
	 • Was the U.S. response to German, Italian, and Japanese aggression in Europe, Africa, and Asia from 1935 to 1941 strategic, unwise, or rash?
	 • Which plan to defeat the Axis Powers would have been more effective?
	   - Roosevelt's plan to invade France across the English Channel
	   - Churchill's indirect approach of advancing northward from the Mediterranean Sea
	   - Stalin's support for opening a western front at the earliest possible time
	 • Which elements of the Allied Powers' plan were reasonable, unreasonable, or rash?
	   - The military campaign against Germany and Japan
	   - The punishment of German and Japanese leaders at war crime trials
	   - The imposition of new governments in Germany and Japan to prevent any further attempt to overturn the international system
	 • Was the Atlantic Charter established by the United States and the United Kingdom effective or ineffective?

Consider how these argumentative questions engage students to critically review historical actions and decisions. Instead of identifying what the decisions were or how they were made, argumentative questions prompt students to critique the appropriateness, effectiveness, and wisdom of these choices. These questions prompt students to develop a deep understanding of these historic ideas, incidents, individuals, and issues.

Conclusion

The correct answer in argumentative questioning lies within the question itself. The correct answer is about the choices made, options given, or positions taken. It's up to the student to defend whether a choice, claim, conclusion, or contention is right. Students also learn not every issue, problem, or situation can be resolved conclusively. Most important, argumentative questions engage students to present their own commentary on critical ideas and issues and to defend and support their viewpoint with valid reasoning and relevant and sufficient evidence.

PROFESSIONAL DEVELOPMENT
How to Develop Good Argumentative Questions That Address Choices, Claims, and Controversies

Objective
Develop good argumentative questions that go beyond teaching and learning for cognitive rigor by addressing differentiation and disposition.

Materials
- College- and career-ready standards adopted by your state
- Curriculum and texts adopted by your school
- Good Questions and Bloom's Taxonomy (Figure 1.2)
- Good Questions and Depth of Knowledge (Figure 1.4)

Procedure
1. Identify the academic standards, texts, and topics that will be addressed as part of the lesson or unit.

2. Identify the central ideas and key details in a text. Use Figure 7.9 to help you phrase good argumentative questions that prompt students to comment upon and critique the logic, reasoning, and validity of claims, conclusions, and contentions made by a text or author.

3. Examine multiple perspectives and points of view about an idea, incident, individual, or issue. Pose good argumentative questions that ask students to examine and evaluate all sides before drawing a conclusion or making a decision.

4. Identify circumstances, issues, problems, and situations that can be answered with *yes* or *no*. Rephrase them into good argumentative questions that ask students to choose *either/or*.

5. Research authentic real-world circumstances, issues, problems, and situations that are considered to be highly complicated and contentious—or wicked. Pose good argumentative questions that ask students to recommend and suggest *what should/how should* these circumstances and situations be addressed or handled.

Figure 7.9   Good Argumentative Questions Generator

DECIDE AND DEFEND	Is		or	
	Was		or	
	Should		or	
	Could		or	
	Would		or	
	Should		or	
	What should be done			
	How should			
	Why should			
	What is needed or necessary			

8

How Do Good Affective Questions Promote Differentiation and Disposition?

You are teaching a unit on processes, rules, and laws in government and society and the civic virtues and democratic principles that define and guide them. Your students are expected to do the following:

- Identify core civic virtues and democratic principles that guide government, society, and communities; analyze ideas and principles contained in the founding documents of the United States; explain how they influence the social and political system; evaluate social and political systems. (C3.D2.Civ.8.3-12)

- Identify the beliefs, experiences, perspectives, and values that underlie their own and others' points of view about civic issues; explain the relevance of personal interests and perspectives, civic virtues, and democratic principles when people address issues in government and civil society; analyze the impact and the appropriate roles of personal interests and perspectives on the application of civic virtues, democratic principles, constitutional rights, and human rights. (C3.D2.Civ.10.3-12)

Your students will respond to the good questions in Figure 8.1.

Teaching and learning for cognitive rigor shifts the instructional focus from solely demonstrating higher levels of thinking (Bloom's Revised Taxonomy) to addressing the extent of student knowledge and understanding (Webb's Depth-of-Knowledge Levels). However, what do we truly want our students to do with all the *stuff* they are learning?

Take a close look at the good questions students are asked about the democratic principles of government and society. We're not asking them to describe what these principles are or explain how and why they define and guide processes and rules. We're not asking them to consider different scenarios or take a position in a debate. What we are asking each student is to express *what are* your *opinions, perspectives, and thoughts*. What we're also asking is for each student to show *how do* you *use* civic virtues and democratic principles and to share *what do* you *think* should be done to address public issues. The instructional focus and summative assessment of these questions is not on how deeply students know and understand these concepts and content. It is on the student's feelings—or dispositions—on these subjects and how each student can express personal attitudes, beliefs, and values clearly. This is known as affective learning—instruction and assessment that asks a student to demonstrate and communicate the depth and extent of *what he does, believes, thinks, feels, or could do* with the knowledge (Krathwohl, Bloom, & Masia, 1964).

Figure 8.1   Good Affective Questions: Government

AFFECTIVE	What is *your* opinion on a particular on a public issue that is currently affecting your community?
	What is *your* perspective on a controversial issue or topic that has been a subject of public debate, discourse, or decision making?
	What are *your* thoughts on how certain global issues have been handled by the United States and international government agencies and officials?
	How do *you* use civic virtues and democratic principles when you interact with others?
	How can *you* ensure you use civic virtues and democratic principles when you interact with others on public matters?
	What virtues and principles do *you* think should be applied and used to address and respond to public issues?

Good affective questions prompt students to examine their opinions and perspectives on the questions instead of concepts or content. The questions also encourage students to show what they can do or how they can, could, would, or will answer a question, address a problem, or accomplish a task.

What Good Affective Questions Do

Good affective questions emphasize personal expression—specifically, how convincingly students can demonstrate and communicate the depth of their personal learning as well as how they feel about what they learned. Such questions prompt students to do the following:

• Convey what they believe, feel, or think about a specific text or topic.

• Express what their opinions, perspectives, or thoughts are about a particular idea, incident, individual, or issue.

• Share what they would do or what they will do given certain conditions or contexts.

• Show how they could or how they would answer a question, address a problem, or accomplish a task.

The way the term *affective* is being used in this chapter is synonymous with *emotional*—an aspect of teaching that is essential but unfortunately not emphasized with standards and assessment-based learning. The dispositions, emotions, and feelings that students are expected to express are found within the Affective Domain of Bloom's Revised Taxonomy that categorizes the following behavioral actions:

• **Receive**—How do *you* acquire, acknowledge, and attend to information and develop understanding of circumstances, experiences, and situations?

• **Respond**—How do *you* respond to ideas, incidents, individuals, and issues and become motivated to go further and learn more about the text or topic?

• **Value**—How do *you* establish and express beliefs, ideals, and a sense of worth about a behavior, experience, object, phenomenon, or problem?

• **Organize**—How do *you* process and synthesize beliefs and ideals into a system of values that may conflict with the perspective of others?

• **Characterize** or internalize—How do *you* develop your system of values into a philosophy or lifestyle you draw upon and use to handle expectations and experiences? (Krathwohl et al., 1964)

Notice what this domain of Bloom's taxonomy addresses—attitudes, emotions, feelings, motivation, philosophy, and values related to learning. Its focus is on the student, not the skill, strategy, or subject. The categories within the taxonomy describe and detail how students individually cope and contend with the ideas and information and how they convey their personal awareness and attitudes about texts and topics on an emotional level, not a cognitive one. The Affective Domain brings a behavioral aspect to rigorous teaching.

Good affective questions promote cognitive rigor by challenging students to demonstrate thinking at Bloom's highest category (create) as they continue to engage and communicate knowledge at the deepest levels of Webb's (DOK-3 and DOK-4). Remember that cognitive rigor superimposes the Cognitive Domain of Bloom's Revised Taxonomy with Webb's Depth-of-Knowledge Level and does not include the Affective Domain of Bloom's taxonomy; however, good affective questions do include this learning dimension. That's why good affective questions emphasize that the instructional focus target is the student by using the pronoun *you*. We want them to demonstrate and communicate how they have personally processed their education and experiences into personal expertise.

Let's take a look at how good affective questions shift the instructional focus from demonstrating thinking and communicating knowledge to expressing and sharing emotions about what is being taught.

Differentiation and Individualization

Affective questions encourage students to share the depth of their learning in their own unique way (Coil, 2004; Tomlinson, 1999; Wormelli, 2007). Consider how the affective questions in Figure 8.2 shift the focus from thinking deeply about the subject to the students and their thoughts about the subject.

Figure 8.2   Creating Affective Questions

ORIGINAL QUESTION	GOOD AFFECTIVE QUESTIONS
How can problems involving multiplication be represented and solved?	How can *you* represent and solve problems involving multiplication?
What is the difference between a hero and an idol?	What do *you* think is the difference between a hero and an idol?
How can rate language be used to describe a ratio relationship between two quantities?	How can *you* use rate language to describe a ratio relationship between two quantities?
How do climate maps provide the following information? • Climate of a region • Precipitation of a region • Meteorological conditions of a region • Climatological changes in a region over a period of time	How could *you* use climate maps to determine the following? • Climate of a region • Precipitation of a region • Meteorological conditions of a region • Climatological changes in a region over a period of time
What caused the transcendentalist movement to come to an end in the United States?	What do *you* think caused the transcendentalist movement to come to an end in the United States?
What could happen if technology were developed to provide humans the ability to choose the traits in organisms?	What do *you* think could happen if technology were developed to provide humans the ability to choose the traits in organisms?
Should Pluto be considered one of the nine planets surrounding the sun, be excluded as one of the nine planets, or be given a special designation?	Do *you* think Pluto should be considered one of the nine planets surrounding the sun, be excluded as one of the nine planets, or be given a special designation?

Notice the shift in the instructional focus in Figure 8.2 is slight but effective. The cognitive rigor questions in the left column are all good questions that promote cognitive rigor. They engage students to think deeply and express their learning at various levels of Bloom's taxonomy and Webb's Depth of Knowledge and challenge students to demonstrate deeper knowledge and thinking.

Do note the emphasis. It's not the student, specific skill, strategy, or subject. Instead, the questions encourage students to share the depth of their knowledge as opinions and perspectives. The responses are authentic and may vary widely because they truly reflect the depth of each individual student's attitude about the topic.

Good affective questions are similar to driving questions because they both use *you* as the pronoun to promote differentiation and individualization. Good driving questions engage students to use their skills and talent to create, design, develop, or produce some kind of artifact (a paper, a plan, a product, a project) that represents the depth of their learning. Affective questions, however, are more intimate and intrapersonal and involve students in personal, active, and authentic education experiences.

Self-Knowledge and Awareness

Affective questions are also similar to good analytical questions in that they expand students' knowledge of the concepts and procedures for transfer and use in a variety of circumstances. However, affective questions extend students' thinking by prompting them to demonstrate how they can personally use different subject-specific skills and strategies to study phenomena and solve problems. Consider how the affective questions in Figure 8.3 shift the instructional focus from understanding and explaining to more practical aspects of learning.

Notice how the expectations of the performance objectives for mathematics in Figure 8.3 address both analytical and affective questions, yet the cognitive rigor focus of each question differs. Good analytical questions target how a subject-specific skill or strategy can be used to attain answers and outcomes. Good affective questions guide students to communicate how they can personally use a specific algorithm, formula, method, or technique to explain their answers.

Conditional and Contextual Knowledge

Affective questions are similar to good hypothetical questions in that they engage students to consider, hypothesize, or imagine *what if*. However, unlike hypothetical questions that engage students to think critically about what could happen or what would happen in a given scenario or situation, affective questions

Figure 8.3   Analytical Questions Versus Affective Questions

COLLEGE- AND CAREER-READY MATH STANDARDS	GOOD ANALYTICAL QUESTIONS	GOOD AFFECTIVE QUESTIONS
Represent and solve problems involving addition and subtraction.	How can addition problems be represented and solved?	How can *you* represent and solve addition and subtraction problems?
Use place value understanding and properties of operations to perform multidigit arithmetic.	How can the following be used to perform multidigit arithmetic? • Place value understanding • Properties of operations	How can *you* use the following to perform multidigit arithmetic? • Place value understanding • Properties of operations
Build fractions from unit fractions.	How can fractions be built from unit fractions?	How can *you* build fractions from unit fractions?
Convert like measurement units within a given measurement system.	How can like measurements within a given system be converted?	How can *you* convert like measurement units within a given measurement system?
Solve real-world and mathematical problems involving area, surface area, and volume.	How can real-world and mathematical problems involving the following be solved? • Area • Surface area • Volume	How can *you* solve real-world and mathematical problems involving the following? • Area • Surface area • Volume
Analyze proportional relationships and use them to solve real-world and mathematical problems.	How can proportional relationships be analyzed and used to solve real-world and mathematical problems?	How can *you* solve real-world and mathematical problems by analyzing and using proportional relationships?
Analyze and solve linear equations and pairs of simultaneous linear equations.	How can the following be analyzed and solved? • Linear equations • Pairs of simultaneous linear equations	How can *you* analyze and solve the following? • Linear equations • Pairs of simultaneous linear equations
Summarize, represent, and interpret data on a single count or measurement variable	How can data be summarized, represented, and interpreted on a single count or measurable variable?	How can *you* summarize, represent, and interpret data on a single count or measurable variable?
Represent complex numbers and their operations on the complex plane.	How can complex numbers and their operations be represented on the complex plane?	How can *you* represent complex numbers and their operations on the complex plane?
Use polynomial identities to solve problems.	How can polynomial identities be used to solve problems?	How can *you* use polynomial identities to solve problems?
Interpret functions that arise in applications in terms of the context.	How can functions that arise in applications in terms of the context be interpreted?	How can *you* interpret functions that arise in applications in terms of the context?
Prove geometric theorems.	How can geometric theorems be proven?	How can *you* prove geometric theorems?

challenge students to think critically about what they could or would do given certain conditions. Consider how the following scenario engages students to express how they could or would address a situation involving forces and motion.

You are teaching a unit on forces and motion. Your students are expected to do the following:

- Apply Newton's Third Law to design a solution to a problem involving the motion of two colliding objects. (NGSS MS-PS2-1)

Your students will respond to the good questions in Figure 8.4.

Figure 8.4   Driving, Hypothetical, and Affective Questions

GOOD DRIVING QUESTION	
What kind of solution could you design to a problem involving the motion of two colliding objects using Newton's Third Law?	
GOOD HYPOTHETICAL QUESTION	GOOD AFFECTIVE QUESTON
How could Newton's Third Law be used to solve a problem involving the motion of two colliding objects?	How could *you* use Newton's Third Law to solve a problem involving the motion of two colliding objects?

Notice the difference in the instructional focus in these questions. The driving question concentrates on what kind of question can be designed to solve a problem using Newton's Third Law. The affective question is more student-centered—how could the student personally use Newton's Third law to find a solution. With this question, the focus is on the student.

Affective questions also ask students how they would or could use what they have learned in a variety of contexts. These questions can also be good driving questions that engage students to create, do, or produce something to address a specific problem in a particular context. Consider the following scenario.

You are teaching a unit about participation and deliberation in civics. Your students are expected to do the following:

- Apply civic virtues and democratic principles in school settings and community settings and working with others. (C3.D2.Civ.7.K-12)

- Follow and use agreed-upon rules for discussion and deliberative processes when making decisions or reaching judgments as a group in multiple settings. (C3.D2. Civ.9.K-12)

Your students will address and respond to the good questions in Figure 8.5.

Figure 8.5   Good Driving Questions: Civil Participation

GOOD DRIVING QUESTION	
How could you address and respond to a particular circumstance, issue, problem, or situation in your school or local community using civic virtues and democratic principles?	
GOOD HYPOTHETICAL QUESTION	**GOOD AFFECTIVE QUESTION**
How could civic virtues and democratic principles be applied in the following scenarios and situations? • School settings • Community settings • Working with others How could agreed-upon rules for discussion and deliberative processes be used when making decisions or reaching judgments as a group in multiple settings?	How could *you* apply civic virtues and democratic principles in the following scenarios and situations? • School settings • Community settings • Working with others How could *you* use agreed-upon rules for discussion and deliberative processes when making decisions or reaching judgments in a group and in multiple settings?

The difference in the instructional focus between the hypothetical and affective questions is clear. The hypothetical questions focus on how the civic virtues and democratic principles *could* be used in multiple settings; affective questions emphasize *how would* each individual student use these virtues and principles in different settings. The driving question is an affective question that asks students how could or would they address a particular issue or problem using the principles of civics and democracy. However, the question is considered more of a driving question because it asks students to do or produce a solution in a particular context.

Perspective and Point of View

Affective questions are also similar to argumentative questions in that they prompt students to make a choice and defend decisions using valid reasoning and sufficient evidence. The response to an affective question, however, is based on personal opinion and driven more by the students' perspectives than facts and logic. Consider how the good affective questions in Figure 8.6 engage and encourage students to express and share their perspectives and points of view on a subject or topic.

Figure 8.6   Comparing Questions: Bad, Good Argumentative, Good Affective

BAD QUESTION	GOOD ARGUMENTATIVE QUESTION	GOOD AFFECTIVE QUESTION
Should reading and math be taught across the curriculum?	Should reading and math be taught and learned across the curriculum, in certain classes, or only during the specific class and time period?	What do *you* think about teaching and learning reading and math across the curriculum?
Does technology make us more alone and isolated?	Does technology make us more isolated from or more connected to people?	What is *your* opinion on whether technology makes us more connected or more isolated?
If football is so dangerous to players, should we be watching it?	Is football dangerous, not dangerous, or no more dangerous than any other athletic competition or sport?	What are *your* thoughts about football being considered dangerous and whether it should be aired on TV?
If you could have any superpower, what would it be?	Would it a blessing or a curse to have a superpower?	Would *you* want a superpower and why?
How will the U.S. economy improve under the next president?	Will the U.S. economy improve, not improve, or stay the same with the next president?	What do *you* think will happen to the U.S. economy with the next president?
Is modern culture ruining childhood?	Is modern culture ruining or improving childhood?	How do *you* feel about the effects of modern culture on childhood?
Is online learning as effective as face-to-face learning?	Which is a better way to learn— online or face-to-face?	Which do *you* think is a better way to learn—online or face-to-face?

Notice the difference between the three types of questions. The first column contains questions that would be considered "bad" because they either direct or limit students' thinking and responses. The argumentative question focuses more on how students can defend their claims based upon using valid reasoning and specific evidence. The affective question response is based upon their opinions and points of view.

Affective questions encourage debate and discussion, but their intent is to present and persuade. The goal is for students to share and explain their ideas and opinions to an audience, perhaps changing the audiences' opinions. Students are expected to respond to the argumentative questions in Figure 8.6 with a claim that either defends or refutes an idea based upon valid reasoning and evidence. Affective questions ask students to share their perspectives and points of view based upon the same criteria along with expertise developed from their education and experience.

How Can We Teach with Good Affective Questions?

Affective questions are highly subjective and student-centric. How students address these questions is based on their personal knowledge and attitude. Their responses will have strong emotional components as they reflect and represent the depth and extent of their knowledge, thinking, and disposition. Students also need to learn how to convey their learning authentically and convincingly and appropriately attend to the perspectives and points of view of others.

To accomplish this, students are encouraged to respond to affective questions as if they were experts in a particular area, subject, or field of study. They are expected to return the respect when their classmates act as experts. All students should be given the flexibility and freedom to express themselves. Remember that good affective questions are about our students and how they process what they have learned. Let's take a look at how good affective questions can be used across the curriculum to encourage this expert approach to texts and topics.

English Language Arts, Fine Arts, Visual Arts

Affective questions turn students into critics or reviewers, judging a text or work based upon its merit, quality, and value. Students are expected to think critically about how the author, artist, or musician uses the craft and the conventions of their discipline in their products. Student responses to affective questions are, however, a personal critique based upon their emotions, perceptions, and even philosophy. Students are also encouraged to defend the claims made by others. Consider how the following good affective questions encourage students to express their opinions and thoughts about *The Adventures of Huckleberry Finn* by Mark Twain.

You are teaching a novel study on *The Adventures of Huckleberry Finn* by Mark Twain. Your students are expected to do the following:

- Read closely to determine what the text says explicitly and to make logical inferences from it; cite specific textual evidence when writing or speaking to support conclusions drawn from the text. (CCSS.ELA-Literacy.CCRA.R.1)

- Determine central ideas or themes of a text and analyze their development; summarize the key supporting details and ideas. (CCSS.ELA-Literacy.CCRA.R.2)

- Analyze the structure of texts, including how specific sentences, paragraphs, and larger portions of the text (e.g., a section, chapter, scene, or stanza) relate to each other and the whole. (CCSS.ELA-Literacy.CCRA.R.5)

- Assess how point of view or purpose shapes the content and style of a text. (CCSS. ELA-Literacy.CCRA.R.6)

- Delineate and evaluate the argument and specific claims in a text, including the validity of the reasoning as well as the relevance and sufficiency of the evidence. (CCSS.ELA-Literacy.CCRA.R.8)

- Write arguments to support claims in an analysis of substantive topics or texts using valid reasoning and relevant and sufficient evidence. (CCSS.ELA-Literacy.CCRA.W.1)

- Draw evidence from literary or informational texts to support analysis, reflection, and research. (CCSS.ELA-Literacy.CCRA.W.9)

- Evaluate a speaker's point of view, reasoning, and use of evidence and rhetoric. (CCSS.ELA-Literacy.CCRA.SL.3)

- Apply knowledge of language to understand how language functions in different contexts, to make effective choices for meaning or style, and to comprehend more fully when reading or listening. (CCSS.ELA-Literacy.CCRA.L.3)

Your students will address the good questions in Figure 8.7.

Figure 8.7   Good Affective Questions: *The Adventures of Huckleberry Finn*

AFFECTIVE	What is *your* opinion about the controversy and criticism over *The Adventures of Huckleberry Finn* by Mark Twain?
	What is *your* perspective on *The Adventures of Huckleberry Finn* as a work of classic literature?
	What are *your* thoughts about the unique structure and style of *The Adventures of Huckleberry Finn*?
	What are *your* thoughts about *The Adventures of Huckleberry Finn* by Mark Twain as a social commentary on antebellum America and the principles and virtues of civilized society?
	What are *your* thoughts about Alan Gribben publishing a version of *The Adventures of Huckleberry Finn* that replaces the racial epithets Twain originally included in the novel with more politically correct or acceptable terms?
	What is *your* opinion about Twain's *The Adventures of Huckleberry Finn* and how readers and society react, regard, and respond to the novel?

Consider the objective of the good affective questions. They are not asking students to conduct a literary analysis of the key ideas and details of *The Adventures of Huckleberry Finn*, or conduct a style analysis of the work, or think critically about how the author integrates ideas. These questions prompt students to express their own ideas and perspectives about the novel. They also ask students to provide their own interpretations of the meaning of certain passages and quotes. Most important, the questions encourage students to express their own opinions about the novel and whether they agree with the comments and criticisms of others. Students do need to support their opinions with valid reasoning and sufficient evidence, despite their review being based upon personal opinion more than analysis and evaluation of the work.

Mathematics

Using affective questions in mathematics shifts the instructional focus to the student and away from mathematical skills and strategies. They encourage students to express how they personally can, could, or would use the math to solve different mathematical and real-world problems. Look back at how the affective questions in Figure 8.3 (p. 127) shift the instructional focus from explaining how subject-specific skills can be generally used to a focus that prompts students to demonstrate how they can personally use a certain method or technique to solve math problems.

Affective questions also encourage students to express their attitudes and perceptions about math and how they personally can transfer and use the concepts and procedures to solve problems. These good questions make math more individualized and emotional by simply asking students what they believe or think would be the best method to solve a particular problem rather than requiring the use of a certain procedure. Consider how the following scenario engages students to choose the mathematical method, strategy, or technique they think would best solve a particular mathematical or real-world problem.

You are teaching a unit on how to perform operations with multidigit whole numbers and with decimals to hundredths. Your students are expected to do the following:

- Find whole-number quotients of whole numbers with up to four-digit dividends and two-digit divisors, using strategies based on place value, the properties of operations, and/or the relationship between multiplication and division. Illustrate and explain the calculation by using equations, rectangular arrays, and/or area models. (CCSS.MATH.CONTENT.5.NBT.B.6)

Your students will address and respond to the good questions in Figure 8.8.

Figure 8.8   Good Affective Questions: Multidigit Whole Numbers and Decimals

AFFECTIVE	Which strategy or strategies would *you* use to find whole-number quotients of whole numbers with up to four-digit dividends and two-digit divisors, and why? • Partial quotients • Place value strategy • Strategies involving the property of operations • Relationship between multiplication and division • Distributive property • Multiplying up • Proportional reasoning • Open arrays • Clusters

A good hypothetical question asks students how a set of mathematical strategies could be used to find whole-number quotients of whole numbers with up to four-digit dividends and with two-digit divisors. Affective questions increase the cognitive rigor and personalize the learning experience by giving students the freedom to decide which strategy they would use. Such an approach demonstrates knowledge and thinking as it fosters differentiation.

Creating good affective questions for math is as easy as adding the pronoun *you* to analytical and hypothetical questions. This simple change extends complexity of thinking and depth of knowledge and incorporates an emotional component into the teaching of math that ultimately increases mathematical competency and confidence.

Science

Good affective questions in science serve three purposes. The first is to prompt students to communicate what kind of model could be developed and used to explain natural events or phenomena. These questions will typically be good driving questions because they engage students to demonstrate their knowledge and thinking through project-based learning (see Chapter 2 to review how to develop good driving questions in science).

The second purpose is to prompt students to think critically and creatively about what they can do with science or how they can use it to explain natural events and phenomena. These are the good questions that engage students to think like scientists who use their deep knowledge about scientific practices to explain our world and the natural forces that occur within it. Consider the following performance objectives in Figure 8.9 and how each is converted into affective questions that encourage students to use scientific methods and principles to explain the world and certain events.

Figure 8.9   Making Affective Questions from Science Standards

COLLEGE- AND CAREER-READY SCIENCE STANDARDS	GOOD AFFECTIVE QUESTIONS
Use observations to describe patterns of what plants and animals (including humans) need to survive. (NGSS-K-LS1-1)	How can *you* use observations to describe patterns of what plants and animals (including humans) need to survive?
Use observations of the sun, moon, and stars to describe patterns that can be predicted. (NGSS-1-ESS1-1).	How can *you* use observations of the sun, moon, and stars to describe patterns that can be predicted?
Use information from several sources to provide evidence that Earth events can occur quickly or slowly. (NGSS-2-ESS1-1)	How can *you* use information from several sources to provide evidence that Earth events can occur quickly or slowly?
Analyze and interpret data from fossils to provide evidence of the organisms and the environments in which they lived long ago. (NGSS-3-LS4-1)	How can *you* analyze and interpret data from fossils to provide evidence of the organisms and the environments in which they lived long ago?
Identify evidence from patterns in rock formations and fossils in rock layers to support an explanation for changes in a landscape over time. (NGSS-4-ESS1-1)	How can *you* identify and use evidence from patterns in rock formations and fossils in rock layers to explain changes in a landscape over time?
Obtain and combine information about ways individual communities use science ideas to protect the Earth's resources and environment. (NGSS-5-ESS3-1)	How can *you* obtain and combine information about ways individual communities use science ideas to protect Earth's resources and environment?

These affective questions engage students to explain these natural happenings and occurrences. The focus is not on the events themselves or even the level of thinking and depth of knowledge. These questions ask students to demonstrate and communicate how they personally can use information and observations, analyze and interpret data or evidence, or apply scientific principles to explain the science behind events and phenomena.

The third purpose of good hypothetical questions is to engage students to share their personal opinions or viewpoints and to participate in debates, dialogues, and discussions about current events and proposed scientific hypotheses and ideas. They also encourage students to comment upon the current state of the natural world and suggest how people might protect natural resources. Affective questions can also expand students' knowledge and extend their thinking. Instead of having students subscribe to a particular perspective, these questions encourage students to examine these topics with a critical eye. As with argumentative questions, affective questions should be worded carefully so students cannot simply answer yes or no or agree or disagree without any explanation or evidence supporting their responses.

History and Social Studies

In history and social studies, affective questions provide students the opportunity to express their perspectives and opinions on key events, individuals, and issues throughout history. These good questions allow students to react to history rather than to simply accept the facts presented in a text or by the teacher. Consider how the following scenario encourages students to draw their own conclusions and generate their own ideas about the influence of and effects following the Industrial Revolution.

You are teaching a unit on how the rise of corporations, heavy industry, and mechanized farming transformed the United States. Your students are expected to do the following:

- Understand the connections among industrialization, the advent of the modern corporation, and material well-being. (NHS.USE6.1.A)

- Create and use a chronological sequence to analyze and evaluate how historical events and developments were shaped by unique circumstances of time and place as well as broader historical contexts. (C3.D2.His.1.3-12)

- Explain why individuals and groups during the same historical period differed in their perspectives and analyze complex and interacting factors that influenced the perspectives of people during different historical eras. (C3.D2.His.4.3-12)

- Explain and analyze multiple and complex causes and effects of events in the past. (C3.D2.His.14.3-12)

- Evaluate the relative influence of various causes of events and developments in the past and distinguish between long-term causes and triggering events in developing a historical argument. (C3.D2.His.15.6-12)

Your students will address the good questions in Figure 8.10.

Notice the depth to which students are expected to express their opinions and perspectives. They are prompted to convey what they believe, feel, or think are the industries, individuals, and innovations that had the greatest influence on the

Figure 8.10   Good Affective Questions: Industrialization

AFFECTIVE	What are *your* thoughts about how the Industrial Revolution affected the United States and the world, both in history and today?
	Which technological breakthrough or innovation that occurred during the Industrial Revolution do *you* think had the greatest effect on the United States, historically and presently?
	Which industrial or financial leader during the Industrial Revolution do *you* believe had the greatest influence on the growth and development of the United States, historically and presently?
	What do *you* think is an existing or emerging business that will expand and grow in the future?
	What do *you* think is the technological innovation that has had the greatest influence on the U.S. economy, workforce, and society, historically and presently?
	What do *you* think will be the next technological innovation that will transform the U.S. economy, workforce, and society?
	Who do *you* think is a modern industrial, corporate, or financial leader who has had a great influence on the U.S. economy, workforce, and society?
	Which industrial, corporate, or financial leader do *you* think will have or continue to have a great influence on the U.S. economy, workforce, and society in the future?

United States. Students are also encouraged to extend their thinking by expressing what they believe, feel, and think are the industries, individuals, and innovations that have affected or will affect the U.S. economy, workforce, and society.

Beyond providing an opportunity for students to express their opinions and perspectives, affective questions guide students to realize that history and civic actions and decisions are not dictated by one specific individual, group, or society. Also, it is entirely appropriate for them to draw and express their own conclusions and share their attitudes, beliefs, and feelings in an authentic way.

Conclusion

Good affective questions specifically seek to have students communicate what they personally can do with their expertise and to share their perspective. Most important, these questions incorporate an essential element of deeper learning, which is the communication of personal ability, attitude, and awareness. Remember to be flexible and give students freedom to express themselves and share their ideas. We're assessing their responses for accuracy and acceptability and teaching them how to express themselves appropriately and authentically.

PROFESSIONAL DEVELOPMENT

How to Develop Good Affective Questions
That Promote Differentiation and Disposition

Objective

Develop good hypothetical questions that go beyond teaching and learning for cognitive rigor by addressing differentiation and disposition.

Materials

- College- and career-ready standards adopted by your state
- Curriculum and texts adopted by your school
- Good Questions and Bloom's Taxonomy (Figure 1.2)
- Good Questions and Depth of Knowledge (Figure 1.4)

Procedure

1. Identify the academic standards, texts, and topics that will be addressed as part of the lesson or unit.

2. Identify the central idea of the text or topic that is being read or reviewed. Use Figure 8.11 to list that central idea next to the question stems that ask students to convey *what do* you *believe, feel,* or *think.*

3. Identify the subject being addressed and the claims or conclusions made by authors, sources, and texts. Write the specific subject or claim next to the good question stems that ask students to express *what is* your *opinion, perspective, point of view,* or *thought.*

4. Review the analytical questions developed and derived from the performance objectives of the academic standards that ask students to determine *how can* [a skill or strategy] *be used* to answer a question, address a problem, or accomplish a task. Rephrase the question to ask students to share *how can* you *use* this subject-specific skill or strategy to study phenomena and solve problems.

5. Review the hypothetical questions developed and derived from the performance objectives of the academic standards that ask students to consider *how could* or hypothesize *how would* [a skill or strategy] *be used* to answer a question, address a problem, or accomplish a task. Rephrase the question to ask students to show *how could* you or *how would* you *use* a certain strategy or skill to address and respond to a circumstance, issue, problem, or situation.

6. Always explicitly tell students that the pronoun referent *you* indicates that the instructional focus is on the student, not the skill, strategy, or subject.

Figure 8.11   Good Affective Questions Generator

CONVEY	What do *you* believe	
	How do *you* feel	
	What do *you* think	
EXPRESS	What is *your* opinion	
	What is *your* perspective	
	What are *your* thoughts	
SHARE	What can *you* create	
	What can *you* design	
	What can *you* develop	
	What can *you* plan	
	What can *you* produce	
SHOW	How could *you*	
	How would *you*	
	What kind of original text could *you* produce	
	What kind of model could *you* develop and use	
	What kind of academic or real-world problem could *you* present	

9

How Do Good Personal Questions Motivate Students to Learn?

You are teaching a unit on the causes and consequences of political revolutions in the 18th and 19th centuries. Your students are expected to do the following:

- Understand how the French Revolution contributed to the transformations in Europe and the world. (NHS.WHE7.1.A)

Your students will address and respond to the good question in Figure 9.1.

Figure 9.1   Good Personal Question: The French Revolution

PERSONAL	What do you want to learn about the French Revolution?

The question in Figure 9.1 challenges students to think critically and express their deeper understanding of the causes and consequences of the French Revolution. It also specifically asks students *what do* you *want to learn about the French Revolution?* This good question will motivate students to take ownership of their learning and provide them with the opportunity to express and share what they personally want to know, understand, and learn about this topic.

Questioning for cognitive rigor requires students to communicate the depth of their learning and to develop questions they want to research, explore, experiment with, or investigate in a unique way.

What a Good Personal Question Does

Good personal questions pique curiosity—specifically, the innate inquisitiveness that leads us to delve deeper into a subject that interests us personally. Good questions embolden students to do the following:

- **Consider** what more you want to learn about concepts and content.
- **Contemplate** what else you could learn about a particular text or topic.
- **Communicate** what you have learned about the subject with the class.
- **Choose** how you want to share what you have learned with the class.

Personal questions come directly from the students, and the cognitive rigor may vary based upon their interest in the subject. Some students may decide to delve deeper into analyzing the knowledge (DOK-1). Some students may choose to examine how the knowledge can be used (DOK-2) or to conduct an investigation to explain why the knowledge can be used to explain a situation (DOK-3). Some students may be adventurous and want to see what else can be done with the knowledge or how else the knowledge can be used (DOK-4). As long as it comes from the students and motivates them to take responsibility for learning, it is a good question.

How Can We Teach Using Good Personal Questions?

The goal for teaching with student-generated personal questions is for students to share their acquired personal knowledge and thinking. Educators become facilitators and oversee how clearly, completely, and creatively the students express themselves. What follows are some tips that will help teachers facilitate the process.

- Present students with the Cognitive Rigor Questions Framework and ask them what *they* want to learn. Give them at least a day to come up with their own good personal question to share with the class. The personal question can be any cognitive rigor question. It can be a good factual, analytical, evaluative, hypothetical, argumentative, or affective question that expects them to research a particular detail, dig deeper into an investigation, examine connections, use imagination, defend a conclusion, and then share what they have learned. As long as the questions come from the students and motivate them to take responsibility for learning, they are good questions. Do not feel compelled to push students to ask a question that engages them to demonstrate thinking at a higher level. Simply let them know you expect a detailed and insightful response.

• Teach students about cognitive rigor and how it promotes higher-level thinking and depth of knowledge. Give them a copy of the good questions in Figure 1.2 and Figure 1.4 as a resource. Then give them the Cognitive Rigor Questions (CRQ) Framework with the HOT question stems (see Appendix A) to help them develop good questions to research and design their presentations. If a student comes up with a good question that will benefit the whole class, praise the student and incorporate it into the exploration of the topic.

• Ensure that all students share their personal questions with the class, in part to help students who may be struggling to develop a question.

• Work together if appropriate. If a student is unable to create a good personal question, ask classmates if they are willing to collaborate.

• Avoid taking offense if a personal question is "Why do we need to learn this?" That question engages students to think critically and practically about the relevance of the content. Students posing that question are expected to provide in-depth and insightful responses that can be supported with textual evidence, personal experience, recorded observations, or scientific research. They cannot simply say, "I don't need to learn this," or "I don't want to learn this."

• Provide time for "show and tell" near the end of the unit for students to present to the class what they have learned. As part of the experience, the students become the teacher and must share and teach the class the depth and extent of what they have learned. This experience engages the students to take personal pride and responsibility in learning and teaches key speaking and listening skills—particularly, how to present knowledge and ideas clearly, comprehensively, correctly, and creatively.

Conclusion

Personal questions shift the dynamics of learning to the students along with the responsibility of teaching the class what they feel is important about a topic. Students are expected to deliver a presentation that is educational, engaging, enlightening, and enjoyable as they help their classmates learn more about the concept or topic. Teaching provides students the opportunity to think deeply and learn how to present their knowledge clearly, completely, and creatively.

How to Motivate Students with Good Personal Questions

Objective

Guide students to pose good personal questions that prompt and encourage them to think deeply, express, and share their learning by asking *what do you want to learn* about the texts and topics being read and reviewed in class.

Materials

- College- and career-ready standards adopted by your state
- Curriculum and texts adopted by your school
- Good Questions and Bloom's Taxonomy (Figure 1.2)
- Good Questions and Depth of Knowledge (Figure 1.4)

Procedure

1. Identify the concept or content that will be taught.

2. Ask students *what do you want to learn* (the last question in the CRQ Framework).

3. Provide students at least 24 hours to develop good personal questions.

4. Have students share their good personal questions, and explain that their responses may be incorporated into the lesson or unit.

5. Allow students to work collaboratively or independently to address and respond to their questions.

6. If students create good personal questions that will benefit the whole class, offer to use those good questions as cognitive rigor questions for the whole class. Give them credit for the question and have them grade their peers' responses with you. You can also work with the student to create scoring criteria and expectations for grading. This way, you're allowing the student to learn and be an instructional leader.

7. Schedule time for students to share their questions and responses as a presentation or during show and tell.

10

How Should Students Address
and Respond to Good Questions?

Throughout this book, you have been given extensive direction and guidance on how to develop good questions that promote cognitive rigor by challenging and engaging students to demonstrate higher-order thinking and communicate depth of knowledge. However, we have not discussed how students should answer these questions or how their answers should be assessed.

That's because good questions are not answered. They are addressed and evaluated based upon how the students respond to the question. Let me explain.

Classroom questioning is typically used to assess knowledge and thinking. Do the students know and understand? Can they do what they have been taught? Can they think deeper about what they are learning? We also assess answers based upon their accuracy (Are they correct or incorrect?) or acceptability (Did the students apply the concept or procedures as explicitly and properly as they were taught?). If students answer the question correctly, we conclude that they must have learned the concept and content. If they go into detail beyond what's expected, then they must have learned the concept or content deeply.

Cognitive rigor, however, is qualitative. It is marked and measured by *how deeply and extensively* students can demonstrate and communicate their learning, not *how much* they know or *how many* questions they can answer correctly. With questioning for cognitive rigor, student responses are evaluated based upon their quality. The quality of a response is marked and measured by the following criteria:

• **Accuracy:** Is the response correct or incorrect? For example, does the student provide a response that is proven to be absolute and irrefutable?

• **Acceptability:** Does the response meet the set criteria or expectations? For example, does the student meet or exceed the standard for addressing the question, or does she respond to the question incompletely or unacceptably?

• **Appropriateness:** Does the response go in depth and in detail? For example, does the student support the response with examples, explanations, and evidence or does the student make a blanket statement or provide the result without explaining *how* or *why*?

• **Authenticity:** Is the response insightful and expressed in the student's unique way? For example, does the response truly reflect and represent the depth and extent of the student's learning, or does he simply repeat or restate the information that he acquired and gathered?

These are the criteria for how responses to good questions should be assessed and evaluated—qualitatively rather than quantitatively. How *good* a response is depends upon how deeply or how extensively a student addresses the subject or topic of a question. For example, suppose you're teaching a book study on *The Outsiders* by S. E. Hinton, and you ask your students to address and respond to the following topical essential question: *How does each character in* The Outsiders *reflect, reject, or respond to the social stereotypes of his or her community and culture?* How *good* a student's response is to this question depends upon the following:

• Does the student respond to the question accurately by defining social stereotypes, distinguishing among the different social stereotypes in *The Outsiders*, identifying the different characters, and describing how they reflected, rejected, and responded to the stereotypes?

• Does the student respond to the question acceptably by addressing all aspects of the question (i.e., reflect, reject, and respond) or only touch upon one part?

• Does the student respond appropriately by providing specific examples from the text and explaining how and why these examples serve as evidentiary support for her response?

• Does the student respond authentically by expressing and sharing ideas, opinions, and perspectives on how the novel's characters reflect, reject, and respond to the social stereotypes of their community and culture?

These guiding questions assess and evaluate student responses based upon quality. The questions cannot be answered with a *yes or no* or even one or two sentences. Good questions expect students to express themselves in depth, in detail, and insightfully. They also require students to address the question and respond using some form of oral, written, creative, or technical expression.

With mathematics, the quality of the response is based upon whether students can solve the problem correctly and explain *how and why* they used the concepts and procedures they are learning clearly, comprehensively, and even creatively.

For example, suppose you ask your students, *How can* you *recognize, generate, and explain why fractions are equivalent?* and present them with fractions and mixed numbers to match or make equivalent. The quality of individual responses to this question depends on the following:

• Does the student respond to the question accurately by defining an equivalent fraction and applying the concept and procedures to make and match the fractions presented?

• Does the student respond to the question acceptably by completing all the problems and showing her work?

• Does the student respond appropriately by providing accurate answers and explaining why each fraction and mixed number pair are equivalent and how he determined equivalency?

• Does the student respond authentically by showing and telling how she personally recognized and generated the equivalent fractions verbally in her own words or visually by using fraction models?

The key to promoting cognitive rigor through classroom questioning is communication. Knowing *what is the correct answer* and showing *how can the answer be attained correctly* is half the battle. Students should also be expected to tell *why this is the answer* and think deeply about *how could* they share knowledge and understanding in detail, in depth, insightfully, and in their own unique way. Here are some ways to encourage students to address and respond to good questions:

• **Show and tell.** Set the expectation that students will be required to demonstrate and communicate—or show and tell—what they are learning. Let them know that responding correctly to *what is the answer* and showing *how can concepts and procedures be used* is only half the battle. Students must also be able to tell *why is this the answer* and think deeply about *how else can concepts and procedures be used.* That's what will be expected of them and also how their learning will be assessed and evaluated.

• **Discourage one-word or one-sentence responses.** Answering *What is Earth* by stating *planet* or *Who is Edgar Allan Poe?* by saying *an author who wrote gothic tales in the 1800s* should not be considered acceptable or appropriate responses. Yes, these responses are accurate, but more detail and depth would be needed for an acceptable and appropriate expression of deep knowledge. Encourage students to describe and explain further. Have them use examples from the text as explanations and evidentiary support.

• **Ask "What do you mean?"** Every time students give an answer in the form of a simple statement, ask them, "What do you mean?" This prompts them to explain *why is this the answer* and elaborate upon *how was the answer attained*. It also challenges them to defend and justify their responses and question their thinking and reasoning. For example, if you ask *what is the relationship between fractions and division* and a student responds, *A fraction is a way to divide numbers,* asking *what do you mean* prompts the student to explain her response and to think about how to phrase the response clearly, correctly, and comprehensively. You can also ask *how do you know* to prompt the student to justify her knowledge.

• **Paraphrase or transcribe information.** Do not permit students to recite, repeat, or restate information explicitly as presented by the text or teacher. They should paraphrase or transcribe the information and cite or credit the source. For example, students should define *what is volume* or describe *where and when did World War II take place* in their own words—not simply copy the text. Having students explain in their own words "encourages a deeper processing of ideas, which can lead to a better understanding of the material"—especially if the students write the information longhand (Mueller & Oppenheimer, 2014).

• **Teach like an expert.** Teachers generally teach students *what is the answer* by presenting the question or problem and showing and telling students how to use concepts and procedures to answer the question correctly. Experts, however, pose the question, present their answer, explain how and why they achieved their outcome or result, and show how it can be applied in different contexts. That's what students need to learn—how to transfer and use knowledge and thinking. To promote deep learning, present students the question or problem with its answer or solution and ask them to examine *how* and *why*. You can show the procedures and prompt them to explain *how is the concept and procedure used*. Then, once they provide an explanation that is accurate, acceptable, appropriate, and authentic, challenge them to investigate and inquire *how else can the concept and procedure be used*.

• **Have students choose their grade.** Unfortunately, some students may not go into the detail and depth necessary. They may feel as if answering the question correctly or the information they provide is "good enough." Although we want our students to go into depth and detail with their responses, we don't want to discourage them or make them feel defensive. Here's a dialogue that I use with students to encourage them to provide more depth and detail in their responses:

Mr. Francis: Is this your answer?
Student: Yes.
Mr. Francis: Is this your final answer?
Student: Yes.
Mr. Francis: Is that your *A* answer?

Student: I think it is.

Mr. Francis: OK. Do you want an A? *(I hope the student will say yes.)*

Student: Yes.

Mr. Francis: If you want an A, why don't you tell me a little more about how you came to this response? However, that's up to you. What you have here is accurate, but your grade is based upon whether the response is acceptable, appropriate, and authentic. So if you want that A, why don't you look into this or tell me how you came to this response? It's up to you.

Notice that instead of telling the student that his response is not "good enough," I ask him to consider and reflect upon the quality of his response by asking what he thinks and for his perception. Using this method means that you're validating the student's response as accurate but challenging and encouraging him to go deeper so that his answer meets all criteria for responding to good questions. You're also suggesting what he should examine and investigate to improve his response. However—and this is key—you're allowing the student to choose whether to expand upon the answer and earn a higher grade. You're teaching the student to delve deeper and giving a life lesson about making good choices and producing high-quality work. If he chooses not to work harder, he needs to accept the grade earned.

Keep in mind that cognitive rigor is qualitative, not quantitative. Promoting cognitive rigor through classroom questioning involves asking good questions that prompt students to think deeply about how they can transfer and use what they are learning. The quality of their responses should be evaluated not only based upon whether they are accurate but also whether they truly express and share the depth of students' learning in an acceptable, appropriate, and authentic manner.

Appendix A

Cognitive Rigor Question Framework

This appendix consists of the Cognitive Rigor Question (CRQ) Framework and the correlating question stems for each type of good question. The framework can be used as a whole or segmented and separated into its individual components and sections to promote cognitive rigor through classroom questioning.

The CRQ Framework categorizes questions based upon their level of complexity. It also maps out how students will process and personalize the information they have acquired and gathered into deep knowledge and thinking over the course of a learning experience.

The four different types of essential questions are universal, overarching, topical, and driving. They provide a comprehensive overview of what students will learn. The universal essential questions address broad and timeless ideas and issues that stretch across the curriculum and beyond the classroom. The overarching questions concentrate on the core ideas and enduring understandings of an academic area or subject. The topical essential questions set the instructional focus and serve as the summative assessment for a lesson or unit. The driving essential question engages students to develop and demonstrate their talent and thinking through project-based, inquiry-based, problem-based, expeditionary, or service learning.

Factual, analytical, and reflective questions challenge students to develop deeper knowledge and understanding of the texts and topics they are reading and reviewing. Factual questions engage students to read and research to build background knowledge. Analytical questions challenge students to examine, experiment with, and explain concepts and procedures. The reflective questions encourage students to investigate and inquire to extend learning and understanding.

The hypothetical, argumentative, affective, and personal questions engage students to process and personalize the deep knowledge they have acquired and developed. Hypothetical questions provide students opportunities to think critically and creatively about how they could transfer and use what they have learned in different academic and real-world contexts. Argumentative questions prompt students to make and defend decisions they can justify and support using their education and experience—or expertise—as evidence and examples. Affective questions encourage students to express and share their attitudes, beliefs, and feelings about texts and topics. Personal questions personalize learning by asking students to pose their own question about the concept or content they personally want to address and share what they have learned with their classmates and peers.

ESSENTIAL	Universal	Who? What?	How? Why?	What causes? What if? What influences?	Is…or…? Does…or…?
	Overarching	How?	Why?		What causes?
	Topical	How? Why? What causes?	What is the effect? What is the impact? What is the influence?	What is the relationship?	
	Driving	What can you create? What can you design? What can you develop? What can you do? How would you innovate? What can you invent?	What can you produce? What kind of plan could you develop? What kind of problem could you present? What kind of text could you produce? How could you develop and use?		
FACTUAL		Who?	What?	Where?	When?
ANALYTICAL		How? Why? How does it happen? How does it work? How is it used? Why does it happen? Why does it work? Why is it used?	What categorizes? What characterizes? What classifies? What distinguishes? What indicates? What are the similarities? What are the differences?	What is the meaning? What is the message? What is the intent? What is the purpose? What does it represent? What does it signify? What does it symbolize?	

REFLECTIVE	What causes? What is the effect? What is the reason? What is the outcome? What is the result? What is the impact? What is the influence?	What is the outcome? What is the pattern? What is the relationship? What is the diagnosis? What are the ways?		
HYPOTHETICAL	What if? What would happen? What could happen?	How could? How would?	How may? How might?	What will? How will?
ARGUMENTATIVE	Is ... or ...? Was ... or ...? Does ... or ...?	Did ... or ...? Could ... or ...? Would ... or ...?	Should ... or ...? Will ... or ...? Which?	
AFFECTIVE	What do *you* believe? How do *you* feel? What do *you* think?	What is *your* opinion? What is *your* perspective? What are *your* thoughts?	How could *you?* How would *you?*	
PERSONAL	What do *you* want to learn?			

Appendix B

Examples of Universal Essential Questions

Good universal essential questions engage students to reflect upon the ethical, philosophical, and existential concerns unearthed by topics, no matter the academic discipline. They can also be helpful when teaching students how to determine the central idea or theme of texts. The following examples can be used to help students develop a broader understanding of ideas and themes.

What is life?	What is death?
What is justice?	What is honor?
What is freedom?	What is beauty?
What is friendship?	What is love?
What is creativity?	What is a hero?
What is courage?	What is a leader?
What is an adult?	What is power?
What is intelligence?	What is happiness?
What is art?	What is reality?
What is success?	What is a community?
What are our inalienable rights?	What does it mean to be "gifted"?
What is the relationship between freedom and responsibility?	What factors shape our values and beliefs?
What is true love?	What is our destiny?
How can language be powerful?	What causes people to lose and regain faith or hope?
What motivates people?	What influences artists, musicians, and writers to compose, craft, and create?

What distinguishes good from evil?	How do we know what we know?
Why do we believe what we believe?	When is it appropriate to challenge the beliefs or values of society?
What causes us to hate?	What drives our decisions?
How can conflict lead to change?	How do beliefs, ethics, or values influence different people's behavior?
How should differences be addressed?	Should people care more about doing the right thing or doing things right?
Should science and technology respect or push the boundaries and laws of nature?	Should freedom ever be restricted or sacrificed for the sake of security?
How could a positive personality trait become a tragic flaw?	How should prejudice and bias be addressed?
Are leaders born or made?	Is humankind inherently good or evil?
Is it better to be loved, feared, or respected?	Is killing justifiable or indefensible?
Is it better to have loved and lost than to have never loved at all?	Is liberty and justice for all possible?
Are humans born civilized or do they learn how to become civilized?	Does practice make perfect?
Is it possible to have culture without art or language?	Does history make leaders or do leaders make history?
Is freedom ever or truly free?	Is censorship ever or never acceptable or right?
Can all problems be solved?	Is a perfect society or world possible?
Does art imitate life or does life influence art?	Do prestige and wealth bring happiness or sorrow?
Should respect be naturally given or must it be earned?	What responsibility do we have to others and ourselves?
Can love happen at first sight or does it need time to develop?	What rights do people have?
How much of something is too much—or not enough?	Which has a bigger influence—heredity or the environment?
How are people influenced, shaped, and transformed by their education and experiences?	How can innocence be "lost"?

Appendix C

Examples of Overarching Essential Questions

Good overarching essential questions address the core ideas and enduring understandings of an academic area or subject. These questions can be examined and investigated at any grade level. They can also be used as benchmark or summative assessments that truly mark and measure students' depth of knowledge and understanding in a particular subject area.

The following examples are good overarching essential questions that have been derived from the performance objectives of college- and career-ready anchor standards and practices.

Good Overarching Essential Questions for Mathematics

These good overarching essential questions address the Standards for Mathematical Practice of the Common Core State Standards (NGACBP & CCSSO, 2010). They mark and measure the deeper conceptual and procedural understanding and expertise students are expected to develop and demonstrate in mathematics.

C.1 Overarching Essential Questions for Mathematics	
MP.1	How can mathematics be used to make sense of problems by determining the meaning of a problem and looking for points into its solution?
MP.2	How can mathematics be used to reason abstractly and quantitatively?
MP.3	How does mathematics involve constructing viable arguments and critiquing the reasoning of others?
MP.4	How can mathematical models be used to explain and solve problems and situations that arise in everyday life, society, and the workforce?
MP.5	How can mathematical tools be used appropriately and strategically to solve a mathematical academic or real-world problem?
MP.6	Why is it important to demonstrate or communicate precision in mathematics?
MP.7	How does mathematics involve looking for and making use of patterns and structure?
MP.8	How does mathematics involve looking for and expressing regularity in repeated reasoning?

Source: Questions adapted from standards in *Common Core State Standards* by NGACBP & CCSSO, 2010, Washington, DC.

Good Overarching Essential Questions for Reading

These good overarching essential questions are derived directly from Reading Anchor Standards of the Common Core State Standards for English Language Arts and Literacy. They clearly define the general and cross-disciplinary literacy understandings and skills students must develop and demonstrate throughout and beyond their K–12 education (NGACBP & CCSSO, 2010).

C.2 Good Overarching Essential Questions for Reading	
KEY IDEAS AND DETAILS	How can what the text says explicitly be determined by reading closely? How can logical inferences be made from texts through close reading? How can textual evidence be cited and used to support conclusions drawn from the text when writing and speaking?
	How can the central ideas or themes of text be determined and summarized? How do the central ideas and themes develop over the course of a text? How do the key details and ideas address and support the central idea and themes of the text?
	How and why do individuals, events, or ideas develop and interact over the course of a text?
CRAFT AND STRUCTURE	How can the meaning of words and phrases be interpreted in the following manner? • Technically • Connotatively • Figuratively How does specific word choice shape the meaning or tone of text?
	How can text and its individual parts be structured? How do the following relate to each other and the text as a whole? • Specific sentences • Paragraphs • Larger portions of the text (e.g. sections, chapters, parts)
	How does point of view or purpose shape the content and style of a text?
INTEGRATION OF KNOWLEDGE AND IDEAS	How can content be integrated and evaluated in diverse media and formats in the following manner? • Verbally • Visually • Quantitatively How can an argument and the specific claims be delineated and evaluated based upon the following? • The validity of the reasoning • The relevancy and sufficiency of the evidence

Source: Questions adapted from standards in *Common Core State Standards* by NGACBP & CCSSO, 2010, Washington, DC.

INTEGRATION OF KNOWLEDGE AND IDEAS— (*continued*)	How do two or more texts address similar themes and topics to build knowledge? What distinguishes the approach two or more authors take to address similar themes and topics to build knowledge?

Good Overarching Essential Questions for Science and Engineering

These good questions address the cross-cutting concepts and science and engineering practices in the Next Generation Science Standards. They can be used to set the comprehensive objectives and outcomes for science instruction and STEM programs in elementary, middle, and high school (NGSS, 2013).

C.3 Good Overarching Questions for Cross-Cutting Concepts in Science and Engineering	
PATTERNS	How can patterns of change be used to identify, sort, analyze, and explain the following? • Natural phenomena • Cause-and-effect relationships • Rates of change • Data trends and results • Make predictions • Designed products (ES/MS) How are macroscopic patterns related to the nature of microscopic and atomic-level structures? (MS) How can graphs and charts be used to identify patterns in data? (MS) How can different patterns do the following? • Be observed at each of the scales at which a system is studied • Provide evidence of causality in explanations of phenomena (HS)
CAUSE AND EFFECT	How are cause-and-effect relationships routinely identified, observed, tested, and used to make change? (ES) How can cause-and-effect relationships be used to predict phenomena in natural or designed systems? (MS) How and why can phenomena have more than one cause? (MS) Why can some cause-and-effect relationships in systems only be described using probability? (MS) Why are relationships classified as causal or correlational, and why does correlation not necessarily imply causation? (MS) How can systems be designed to cause a desired effect? (HS) How and why can cause-and-effect relationships be suggested and predicted for complex natural and human designed systems by examining what is known about small-scale mechanisms within the system? (HS)

Source: Questions adapted from standards in *Next Generation Science Standards: For States, by States* by NGSS Lead States, 2013, Washington, DC.

(*continued*)

CAUSE AND EFFECT— (*continued*)	Why is empirical evidence required to differentiate between cause and correlation and make claims about specific causes and effects? (HS)
SCALE, PROPORTION, QUANTITY	How can natural objects exist from the very small to the immensely large? (ES) How are standard units used to measure and describe physical quantities such as the following? • Weight • Time • Temperature • Volume (ES) How can the following phenomena be observed at various scales using models to study systems that are too large or too small? • Time • Space • Energy (MS) How do proportional relationships among different types of quantities provide information about the magnitude of properties and processes? (MS) Why can phenomena that can be observed at one scale not be observable at another scale? (MS)
SYSTEMS AND SYSTEM MODELS	How can a system be described in terms of its components and interactions? (ES) How can models be used to represent and explain systems and the following interactions within them? • Inputs, processes, and outputs • Energy and matter flows (MS) How can systems interact with other systems by having subsystems or being a part of larger complex systems? (MS) Why must the boundaries and initial conditions of a system being investigated or described be defined? (HS) How can models be used to simulate systems and interactions within and between systems at different scales? (HS)
ENERGY AND MATTER	How can energy be transferred in various ways and between objects? (ES) How can energy take different forms? (MS) How can the transfer of energy be tracked as energy flows through a designed or natural system? (MS) How can matter be transported into, out of, and within systems? (ES) How and why can matter be conserved in physical and chemical processes due to the conservation of atoms? (MS) How does the transfer of energy drive the motion or cycling of matter? (MS) Why are atoms not conserved but the total number of protons plus neutrons is conserved in nuclear processes? (HS) How and why is the total amount of matter and energy in a closed system conserved? (HS) How and why can changes of energy and matter in a system be described in terms of energy and matter flows into, out of, and within that system? (HS) How and why can energy not be destroyed but can move between places, objects, fields, and systems? (HS)

STRUCTURE AND FUNCTION	What is the relationship between the stability and shape of natural structures and designed objects and their function(s)? (ES)
	How can structures be designed to serve particular functions and by taking into account properties of different materials and how materials can be shaped and used? (MS)
	How can complex and microscopic structures be visualized, modeled, and used to describe how their function depends upon the relationships among its parts? (MS)
	How can complex natural structures/systems be analyzed to determine how they function? (MS)
	Why does investigating or designing new systems and structure require the following to reveal its function or solve a problem? • Detailed examination of the properties of different materials • The structures of different components • The connections of components (HS)
STABILITY AND CHANGE	Why do things change slowly or rapidly? (ES)
	How can explanations of stability and change in natural or designed systems be constructed by examining the changes over time and forces at different scales? (MS)
	How can small changes in one part of a system cause large changes in another part? (MS)
	How can stability be disturbed by either sudden events or gradual changes that accumulate over time? (MS)
	How does science involve constructing explanations of why things change and how they remain stable? (HS)
	How can systems be designed for greater or lesser stability? (HS)
	How can feedback (positive or negative) stabilize or destabilize a system? (HS)
ENGINEERING, TECHNOLOGY, AND APPLICATIONS OF SCIENCE	Why is knowledge of relevant scientific concepts and research findings important in engineering? (ES)
	How can science discoveries about the natural world lead to new and improved technologies developed through the engineering design process? (ES)
	How do people's needs, wants, and demands for new and improved technologies change over time? (ES)
	How do engineers improve existing technologies or create new ones to increase benefits, decrease known risks, and meet societal demands? (MS)
	How have engineering advances led to important discoveries in virtually every field of science? (MS)
	How have scientific discoveries led to the development of entire industries and engineering systems? (MS)
	How are the uses of technologies and any limitations on their use driven by the following? • Individual or societal needs, desires, and values • The findings of scientific research • Differences in such factors as climate, natural resources, and economic conditions (MS)
	How does technology use vary from region to region and over time? (MS)
	How do technologies extend the measurement, exploration, modeling, and computational capacity of scientific investigations? (MS)
	How does all human activity draw on natural resources, and why do they have both short- and long-term consequences that can be positive as well as negative for the health of people and the natural environment? (MS)
	How does science and engineering complement each other in the cycle known as research and development? (HS)

(continued)

NATURE OF SCIENCE	Why do most scientists and engineers work in teams? (ES)
	How does science affect everyday life? (ES)
	How does science assume that objects and events in natural systems occur in consistent patterns that are understandable through measurement and observation? (MS)
	How does science assume the universe is a vast single system in which basic laws are consistent? (MS)
	Why are science findings limited to questions that can be answered with empirical evidence? (MS)
	How can scientific knowledge describe the consequences of actions but not necessarily prescribe the decisions that society makes and takes? (MS)
	What influence do advances in technology and progress of science have on each other? (MS)
	How are scientists and engineers guided by the following habits of mind? • Intellectual honesty • Tolerance of ambiguity • Skepticism • Openness to new ideas (MS)
	How and why does science assume that the universe is a vast single system in which basic laws are consistent? (HS)
	How and why does modern civilization depend on major technological systems? (HS)

Good Overarching Essential Questions for Social Studies

These good overarching questions are derived from academic standards and performance objectives included in the C3 Framework for State Social Studies Standards. They address the key instructional focus of social studies courses—civics, economics, geography, and history. They are also used to foster and promote civic, global, historical, geographical, and economic literacy (NCSS, 2013).

C.4 Good Overarching Essential Questions for Social Studies	
CIVICS	Why is it important for citizens to understand law, politics, and government?
	What are the principles that guide official institutions such as legislatures, courts, and government agencies?
	What are the virtues that citizens should use when they interact with each other on public matters?
	What are the processes and rules by which groups of people make decisions, govern themselves, and address public problems?

Source: Questions adapted from standards in *The College, Career, and Civic Life (C3) Framework for Social Studies State Standards: Guidance for Enhancing the Rigor of K–12 Civics, Economics, Geography, and History* by NCSS, 2013, Silver Spring, MD.

ECONOMICS	How does economic decision making involve setting goals and identifying the resources available to achieve those goals?
	How can people voluntarily exchange goods and services when both parties expect to gain as a result of the trade?
	How do markets exist to facilitate the exchange of goods and services?
	What influence do changes in the amounts and qualities of human capital, physical capital, and natural resources have on current and future economic conditions and standards of living?
	What influence do markets working together have on economic growth and fluctuations?
	What causes and affects economic globalization?
GEOGRAPHY	How is creating maps and other geographical representations an essential and enduring part of seeking new geographic knowledge that is personally and socially useful, and how can that be applied in making decisions and solving problems?
	How are interactions between humans and the environment essential aspects of human life in all societies at local-to-global scales, in specific places, and across broad regions?
	What influence does location have on the culture and types of interactions that occur?
	What is the relationship among Earth's human and physical systems?
	How is the size, composition, distribution, and movement of human populations fundamental to active features on Earth's surface?
	What influence does the expansion and redistribution of the human population have on patterns of settlement, environmental changes, and resource use?
	What impact does political, economic, and technological change sometimes have on population size, composition, and distribution?
	How do global interconnections occur in both human and physical systems?
HISTORY	How does chronological reasoning require understanding the processes of change and continuity to assess the similarities and differences between the past and present?
	How is history interpretive and shaped by a variety of perspectives and points of view that may differ and change over time?
	How is historical inquiry based on materials from the past that can be studied and analyzed?
	How does historical thinking involve using evidence and reasoning to draw conclusions about probable causes and effects, recognizing that these are multiple and complex?

Appendix D

Argumentative Questions for Wicked Problems and Impossible Projects

Wicked problems and impossible projects are complicated by nature because of the many components, factors, individuals, and resources affected and involved. They promote cognitive rigor by providing students with the opportunity to demonstrate and communicate their knowledge and thinking at the highest level of Bloom's taxonomy (analyze, evaluate, create) and deepest levels of Webb's model (strategic and extended thinking). Here are examples of good questions our students can respond to using the deeper knowledge and thinking they have acquired and developed.

How should global climate change be addressed?	What should be done to reduce crime?
How should issues regarding scientific and technological development be addressed?	How powerful should governments and nations be?
What needs to be done to address pollution?	What needs to be done to address water deficits and droughts?
Why should the federal and state tax systems be reviewed?	How should issues related to poverty be handled?
How should immigration be handled?	How should nations address and respond to global conflicts and issues?

What would be a good national immigration policy?	What needs to be done for an organization to develop and prosper?
What should be the consequences for someone who breaks the law based on moral convictions?	How should international drug trafficking be handled?
What should be done about rising healthcare costs?	What needs to be done to ensure natural resources do not become depleted?
How should nations address and respond to epidemics caused by plague?	How should criminals be punished for their crimes?
Why should drugs be legalized or remain illegal?	How should the gap between social classes be addressed?
Who should have the right or not be granted the right to keep and bear arms?	Why should animal testing be banned, permitted, or regulated?
What needs to be done to address deforestation?	Why should stem cell research be permitted or forbidden?
What needs to be done to manage the increasing rate of extinction?	How should schools be held accountable?
What needs to be done to maintain or improve race relations?	How responsible should a government be for the welfare and security of its citizens?
What needs to be done to increase maritime safety?	How should domestic and global terrorism be addressed?
What needs to be done to ensure a balance between civil liberty and national security?	How should children be educated?
How should a nation invest its efforts and funding?	

References

Anderson, L. W., & Krathwohl, D. R. (2001). *A taxonomy for learning, teaching, and assessing: A revision of Bloom's taxonomy of educational objectives.* New York: Addison Wesley Longman.

Anderson, R. C., & Pearson, P. D. (1984). A schema-theoretic view of basic processes in reading. In P. D. Pearson (Ed.), *Handbook of reading research* (pp. 255–292). New York: Longman.

Black, J., & MacRaild, D. (2007). *Studying history* (3rd ed.). New York: Palgrave.

Blackburn, B. R. (2008). *Rigor is NOT a four-letter word.* Larchmont, NY: Eye on Education.

Bloom, B. S., Krathwohl, D. R., & Masia, B. B. (1964). *Taxonomy of educational objectives: The classification of educational goals.* New York: David McKay.

Britannica Digital Learning. (2014). *Teaching argumentation and reading for evidence.* Chicago: Encyclopaedia Britannica. Retrieved from http://info.eb.com/wp-content/uploads/2014/08/WP_RdgEvid.pdf

Coil, C. (2004). *Standards-based activities and assessments for the differentiated classroom.* Marion, IL: Pieces of Learning.

Conley, D. T. (2005). *College knowledge: What it really takes for students to succeed and what we can do to get them ready.* San Francisco: Jossey-Bass.

Cunningham, R. T. (1987). What kind of question is that? In W. W. Wilen (Ed.), *Questions, questioning techniques, and effective teaching* (pp. 67–94). Washington, DC: National Education Association.

Dillon, J. T. (1988). *Questioning and teaching: A manual of practice.* Eugene, OR: Teachers College Press.

Dobson, M. (2013). *Project: Impossible: How the great leaders of history identified, solved and accomplished the seemingly impossible—and how you can, too!* Oshawa, ON, Canada: Multi-Media Publications.

Friedman, M. (2005). *The world is flat: A brief history of the 21st century.* New York: Picador.

Gall, M. D. (1970). The use of questions in teaching. *Review of Educational Research, 40*(5), 707–721.

Graff, G. (2003). *Clueless in academe: How schooling obscures the life of the mind.* New Haven, CT: Yale University Press.

Harvard-Smithsonian Center for Astrophysics. (2014, Sept. 22). "Is Pluto a planet? The votes are in." (Press Release No. 2014-25). Cambridge, MA: Author.

Hess, K. K. (2013). *A guide for using Webb's depth of knowledge with Common Core State Standards.* Center for College and Career Readiness.

Hess, K. K., Carlock, D., Jones, B., & Walkup, J. W. (2009a). *Cognitive rigor: Blending the strengths of Bloom's taxonomy and Webb's depth of knowledge to enhance classroom-level processes.* Dover, NH: National Center for Assessment.

Hess, K. K., Carlock, D., Jones, B., & Walkup, J. W. (2009b). *What exactly do "fewer, clearer, and higher standards" really look like in the classroom? Using a cognitive rigor matrix to analyze curriculum, plan lessons, and implement assessments.* Dover, NH: National Center for Assessment. Retrieved from http://schools.nyc.gov/NR/rdonlyres/D106125F-FFF0-420E-86D9-254761638C6F/0/HessArticle.pdf

Hutchings, M. (n.d.). *Introduction to mathematical arguments.* Berkley: University of California Berkley. Retrieved from https://math.berkeley.edu/~hutching/teach/proofs.pdf

International Astronomical Union. (2006, August). Resolution 5A, Designation of a Planet. *IAU General Assembly: Result of the IAU Resolution Votes.* Presented at 26th General Assembly for the International Astronomical Union, Prague. Retrieved from http://www.iau.org/news/pressreleases/detail/iau0603/

Jonassen, D. H., & Hung, W. (2008). All problems are not equal: Implications for problem-based learning. *Interdisciplinary Journal of Problem-Based Learning, 2*(2). Retrieved from http://docs.lib.purdue.edu/ijpbl/vol2/iss2/4/

Kintsch, W. (1998). *Comprehension: A paradigm for cognition.* New York: Cambridge University Press.

Kintsch, W., & van Dijk, T. A. (1978). Toward a model of text comprehension and production. *Psychological Review, 85*(5), 363–394. Retrieved from http://someya-net.com/104-IT_Kansai_Initiative/Towards_Model_1978.pdf

Kolko, J. (2012). *Wicked problems: Problems worth solving.* Dallas, TX: Austin Center for Design. Retrieved from https://www.wickedproblems.com/1_wicked_problems.php

Krathwohl, D. R. (2002, Autumn). A revision of Bloom's taxonomy: An overview. *Theory into Practice, 41*(4), 212–218.

Krathwohl, D. R., Bloom, B. S., & Masia, B. B. (1964). *Taxonomy of educational objectives: The classification of educational goals [handbook II]: Affective domain.* New York: David McKay.

Marzano R. J., & Simms, J. A. (2013). *Vocabulary for the common core.* Bloomington, IN: Marzano Research.

McConachie, S., Hall, M., Resnick, L., Ravi, A. K., Bill, V. L., Bintz, J., & Taylor, J. A. (2006). Task, text, and talk. *Educational Leadership, 64*(2), 8–14. Retrieved from http://www.ascd.org/publications/educational-leadership/oct06/vol64/num02/Task,-Text,-and-Talk@-Literacy-for-All-Subjects.aspx

McKeown, M. G., Beck, I. L., & Apthorp, H. S. (2010). *Examining depth of processing in vocabulary lessons.* Poster talk presented at the American Educational Research Association Conference, New Orleans, LA.

Mueller, P., & Oppenheimer, D. (2014). The pen is mightier than the keyboard: Advantages of longhand over laptop note taking. Available: https://sites.udel.edu/victorp/files/2010/11/Psychological-Science-2014-Mueller-0956797614524581-1u0h0yu.pdf

National Center for History in the Schools. (1996). National standards for history: Basic edition. Los Angeles: Author. Retrieved from http://www.nchs.ucla.edu/history-standards

National Coalition for Core Arts Standards. (2015). *National core arts standards: A conceptual framework for arts learning.* Dover, DE: Author. Retrieved from http://nationalartsstandards.org/

National Council for the Social Studies. (2013). *The college, career, and civic life (C3) framework for social studies state standards: Guidance for enhancing the rigor of K–12 civics, economics, geography, and history.* Silver Spring, MD: Author.

National Governors Association Center for Best Practices, Council of Chief State School Officers. (2010). *Common Core State Standards.* Washington, DC: Author.

NGSS Lead States. (2013). *Next generation science standards: For states, by states*. Washington, DC: National Academies Press.

Partnership for 21st Century Learning. (2015). *P21 framework definitions*. Washington, DC: Author. Retrieved from http://www.p21.org/our-work/p21-framework

Raths, L. E., Wasserman, S., Jonas, A., & Rothstein, A. (1986). *Teaching for thinking: Theory, strategies, and activities for the classroom* (2nd ed.). New York: Teachers College Press.

Rittel, H. W. J., & Webber, M. M. (1973). Dilemmas in a general theory of planning. *Policy Sciences, 4*(2), 155–169. Retrieved from http://www.uctc.net/mwebber/Rittel+Webber+Dilemmas+General_Theory_of_Planning.pdf

Rose, M. (1989). *Lives on the boundary*. New York: Viking.

Schmoker, M. (2011). *Focus: Elevating the essentials to radically improve student learning*. Alexandria, VA: ASCD.

Shanahan, T., & Shanahan, C. (2012). What is disciplinary literacy and why does it matter? *Topics in Language Disorders, 32*(1), 7–18. Retrieved from http://alliedhealth.ceconnection.com/files/TLD0112A-1337958951687.pdf;jsessionid=9DC7CE49896192D77C1AA79E8AF6D875.

Shuttleworth, M. (2009, Sept. 20). Establishing cause and effect [blog post]. Retrieved from *Explorable Psychology Experiments* at https://explorable.com/cause-and-effect

Stahl, K. A. D., & Stahl, S. A. (2012). Young word wizards! Fostering vocabulary development in preschool and primary education. In E. J. Kame'enui & J. F. Baumann (Eds.), *Vocabulary instruction: Research to practice* (2nd ed., pp. 72–92). New York: Guilford Press.

Tomlinson, C. A. (1999). *The differentiated classroom: Responding to the needs of all learners*. Alexandria, VA: ASCD.

Trilling, B., & Fadel, C. (2009). *21st century skills: Learning for life in our times*. San Francisco: Jossey-Bass.

Trochim, W. M. K. (2006). Establishing cause and effect. *The Research Methods Knowledge Base* (2nd ed). Retrieved from http://www.socialresearchmethods.net/kb/causeeff.php

Vacca, R. (2002). From efficient decoders to strategic readers. *Educational Leadership, 60*(3), 6–11. Retrieved from http://www.ascd.org/publications/educational-leadership/nov02/vol60/num03/From-Efficient-Decoders-to-Strategic-Readers.aspx

Wagner, T. (2014). *The global achievement gap: Why even our best schools don't teach the new survival skills our children need . . . and what we can do about it* (2nd ed). New York: Basic Books.

Walkup, J. W. & Jones, B. (2014, June 16). Developing rigorous lesson plans (using Bloom's knowledge dimension) [blog post]. Retrieved from *Cognitive Rigor to the Core!* at http://cognitiverigor.blogspot.com/2014/06/does-oklahoma-really-need-to-rigor-ize_16.html

Webb, N. (1997). Criteria for alignment of expectations and assessments on mathematics and science education. (Research Monograph No. 6). Washington, DC: Council of Chief State School Officers. Retrieved from http://facstaff.wceruw.org/normw/WEBBMonograph/criteria.pdf

Webb, N. (2002). "Depth of knowledge levels for four content areas." (Unpublished). Retrieved from http://www.hed.state.nm.us/uploads/files/ABE/Policies/depth_of_knowledge_guide_for_all_subject_areas.pdf

Wiggins, G., & McTighe, J. (2005). *Understanding by design* (expanded 2nd ed.). Alexandria, VA: ASCD.

Wood, N. (2007). *Perspectives on argument* (5th ed.). New York: Pearson.

Wormelli, R. (2007). *Differentiation: From planning to practice*. Portland, ME: Stenhouse.

Index

Note: The letter *f* following a page number denotes a figure.

About the Author

Erik M. Francis is the owner and lead professional education specialist for Maverik Education LLC, providing professional development, guidance, and support in teaching and learning for cognitive rigor. He consults on the development, implementation, evaluation, and compliance of Title I programs funded under the Elementary and Secondary Education Act of 1965. He presents professional development seminars at conferences hosted by ASCD, the College Board, Learning Forward, the New Teacher Center, the Association for Middle Level Educators, and the Southern Regional Education Board. Erik has also been a featured speaker at education conferences that addressed gifted education, charter schools, Title I, English language learners, dropout prevention, and social work. He works closely with K–12 schools to develop active and authentic teaching and learning experiences that address the cognitive rigor of college- and career-ready standards.

Erik has been an educator for more than 20 years, working as a middle and high school English language arts and math teacher, a site administrator, and an education program specialist in the Title I unit of a state education agency. He is also a featured presenter for the Education Development and Support Program offered through Grand Canyon University. He holds a master's of science in Film and Television Production and Management from the S. I. Newhouse School of Public Communications at Syracuse University and a master's in Education Leadership from Northern Arizona University. Erik's bachelor of arts in Rhetoric and Communication is from the State University of New York, Albany.

Erik lives with his wife and children in Phoenix. For more information, visit www.maverikeducation.com or contact him at maverik@maverikeducation.com.

Related ASCD Resources: Standards

At the time of publication, the following ASCD resources were available (ASCD stock numbers appear in parentheses). For up-to-date information about ASCD resources, go to www.ascd.org. You can search the complete archives of *Educational Leadership* at http://www.ascd.org/el.

Print Products

Common Core Standards for Elementary Grades 3–5 Math & English Language Arts: A Quick-Start Guide by Amber Evenson, Monette McIver, Susan Ryan, Amitra Schwols, and John Kendall (#113015)

Common Core Standards for Elementary Grades K–2 Math & English Language Arts: A Quick-Start Guide by Amber Evenson, Monette McIver, Susan Ryan, Amitra Schwols, and John Kendall (#113014)

Common Core Standards for High School English Language Arts: A Quick-Start Guide by Susan Ryan, Dana Frazee, and John Kendall (#113010)

Common Core Standards for High School Mathematics: A Quick-Start Guide by Amitra Schwols, Kathleen Dempsey, and John Kendall (#113011)

Common Core Standards for Middle School English Language Arts: A Quick-Start Guide by Susan Ryan, Dana Frazee, and John Kendall (#113012)

Common Core Standards for Middle School Mathematics: A Quick-Start Guide by Amitra Schwols, Kathleen Dempsey, and John Kendall (#113013)

Understanding Common Core State Standards by John S. Kendall (#112011)

For more information: send e-mail to member@ascd.org; call 1-800-933-2723 or 703-578-9600, press 2; send a fax to 703-575-5400; or write to Information Services, ASCD, 1703 N. Beauregard St., Alexandria, VA 22311-1714 USA.

THE WHOLE CHILD

The ASCD Whole Child approach is an effort to transition from a focus on narrowly defined academic achievement to one that promotes the long-term development and success of all children. Through this approach, ASCD supports educators, families, community members, and policymakers as they move from a vision about educating the whole child to sustainable, collaborative actions.

Now That's a Good Question! relates to the **engaged** and **challenged** tenets.

For more about the ASCD Whole Child approach, visit **www.ascd.org/wholechild.**

WHOLE CHILD
TENETS

1 **HEALTHY**
Each student enters school healthy and learns about and practices a healthy lifestyle.

2 **SAFE**
Each student learns in an environment that is physically and emotionally safe for students and adults.

3 **ENGAGED**
Each student is actively engaged in learning and is connected to the school and broader community.

4 **SUPPORTED**
Each student has access to personalized learning and is supported by qualified, caring adults.

5 **CHALLENGED**
Each student is challenged academically and prepared for success in college or further study and for employment and participation in a global environment.

LEARN. TEACH. LEAD.